A Guitarist's Grimoire: Unlocking the Secrets of Creating a Musical Diary to Master Guitar Composition

University Scholastic Press

Copyright © 2024 by University Scholastic Press

TABLE OF CONTENTS

INTRODUCTION

In the vast realm of musical creation, where notes weave together to form intricate tapestries of sound, the journey of a guitarist is both an art and a quest for self-expression. *A Guitarist's Grimoire: Unlocking the Secrets of Creating A Musical Diary To Master Guitar Composition* invites you on an immersive exploration into the heart of musical craftsmanship. This literary companion seeks to unveil the alchemy of guitar composition, delving into the transformative power of a personalized musical diary.

The opening chapter of the book lays the foundation with a focus on *Creating a Musical Diary*. Here, you embark on a journey to understand the significance of a musical diary as a conduit for artistic evolution. The narrative unfolds to explore the various dimensions of the diary, unraveling its potential to serve as a compass for the guitarist's creative odyssey. Aspiring musicians and seasoned players alike will find invaluable insights into the pivotal role a musical diary plays in shaping one's artistic identity.

Chapters like, *Approaches and Best Practices For Your Musical Diary* and *Your Musical Diary Entries*, delve into the practical aspects of maintaining a musical diary. From time-tested methodologies to hands-on techniques, these chapters provide a roadmap for crafting a diary that evolves alongside the guitarist's musical prowess. By demystifying the process, the book empowers you to forge a personalized connection with their instrument and compositions.

Sources of Inspiration and Ideas introduces a treasure trove of muse-inducing techniques, encouraging guitarists to tap into diverse wellsprings of creativity. From the ethereal landscapes of nature to the intricacies of human emotions, this chapter provides a myriad of avenues for artists to explore, ensuring that inspiration becomes an abundant resource rather than a fleeting moment.

Documenting Dreams and Aspirations takes the exploration a step further, inviting you to infuse your own musical diary with personal narratives and aspirations. By intertwining dreams with chords, you not only create a sonic memoir but also gain a deeper understanding of your own artistic purpose. This section serves as a catalyst for introspection, fueling the passion that propels musical expression.

Visual Elements To Include In Your Musical Diary opens a new dimension of creativity, emphasizing the synergy between sight and sound. From sketches to symbols, this chapter illuminates the power of visual representation in enhancing the guitarist's compositional journey. By embracing the visual language, you can enrich your musical diary with a unique and resonant aesthetic.

The final chapters, *Using the Diary as a Source for Your Composition*, bring the narrative full circle, offering practical guidance on translating diary entries into fully-fledged compositions. Here, the book becomes a bridge between introspection and public expression, providing the tools and insights necessary for you to share your musical stories with the world.

In *A Guitarist's Grimoire*, you embark on a transformative expedition, where the strings of your guitar become a medium for self-discovery and artistic revelation. This comprehensive guide not only demystifies the secrets of guitar composition but also empowers musicians to unlock their unique voice within the symphony of creative expression.

University Scholastic Press

CREATING YOUR MUSICAL DIARY

CHOOSE AN ANALOG OR DIGITAL PLATFORM

Choose a dedicated notebook, journal, or a digital platform (such as a note-taking app) to serve as your musical diary. Ensure it's easily accessible for regular updates.

Using analog tools and digital tools for creating a musical diary for guitar composition each has its own set of pros and cons. The choice between the two depends on personal preferences, workflow, and the desired outcome.

Pros and Cons for Analog And Digital Tools

<u>ANALOG TOOLS</u>
Pros:
Tactile Experience: Analog tools, such as physical notebooks, provide a tangible and tactile experience. Writing down musical ideas on paper can feel more connected and personal.

Reduced Distractions: Analog tools generally lack the distractions that come with digital devices, helping you focus solely on your musical ideas without the temptation of checking emails or notifications.

No Technical Dependencies: There's no need for power, software updates, or compatibility issues. Analog tools are simple and always ready to use.
Cons:

Limited Editing Options: Corrections and revisions can be more challenging with analog tools compared to digital ones. This can slow down the creative process and may lead to a loss of some ideas during editing.

Less Integration: Analog tools may not easily integrate with other digital tools or software used in the music production process.

<u>DIGITAL TOOLS</u>

Pros:

Versatility: Digital tools offer a wide range of options for recording, editing, and arranging music. You can easily experiment with different sounds, effects, and arrangements.

Efficiency: Editing and rearranging musical ideas is much quicker in a digital environment. You can cut, copy, paste, and make precise adjustments effortlessly.

Integration: Digital tools can seamlessly integrate with other software and equipment used in the music production process, creating a more streamlined workflow.

Cons:

Technical Challenges: Digital tools may be subject to technical issues such as software glitches, compatibility problems, or hardware malfunctions, potentially disrupting the creative process.

Learning Curve: Some digital audio workstations (DAWs) and software can have a steep learning curve, especially for beginners, which might initially slow down the creative process.

Ultimately, the choice between analog and digital tools depends on personal preferences, workflow preferences, and the specific goals of the musician. Many artists even use a combination of both, leveraging the strengths of each to enhance their creative process.

Choose a method that aligns with your preferences and ensures ease of use.

ANALOG MUSICAL DIARY

Notebook or Journal

A dedicated notebook or journal is a classic choice. Choose one with good paper quality and a size that suits your writing style. A physical notebook allows for a tangible connection to your creative process.

Choosing a dedicated notebook or journal for a musical diary is a personal decision, and factors such as paper quality, size, and binding style can significantly impact your writing experience.

Here are some considerations when deciding to choose a notebook or journal for your musical diary:

Paper Quality: High-quality paper can enhance the writing experience, especially if you plan to use various writing instruments like pens, pencils, or markers. It can prevent bleed-through and feathering.

Recommendation: Look for notebooks with acid-free, archival-quality paper. A paper weight of around 70-100 gsm is often suitable for general use.

Size: Choosing the right size depends on your writing style and whether you prefer portability or a larger canvas for your musical ideas.

Recommendation: Consider a size that feels comfortable for jotting down musical notations and ideas. Common sizes include A5 (5.8 x 8.3 inches) and A4 (8.3 x 11.7 inches).

Tangible Connection: A physical notebook provides a tangible and personal connection to your creative process. The act of writing by hand can stimulate creativity and enhance the feeling of ownership over your musical ideas.

Recommendation: Consider the aesthetics and feel of the notebook cover and the overall design. Choose something that resonates with your personal style.

Compactness: Notebooks are often more compact and portable, making them convenient for on-the-go note-taking and quick jotting down of ideas.

Text-Centric: Notebooks may be more text-centric, making them suitable for musicians who focus primarily on written notations and textual descriptions.

Brand Recommendations:

Moleskine: Moleskine notebooks are known for their smooth paper and durable covers. They offer a variety of sizes and formats suitable for different preferences.

Leuchtturm1917: This brand offers notebooks with numbered pages, a table of contents, and a sturdy build. They are available in various sizes and have excellent paper quality.

Field Notes: If you prefer a smaller, pocket-sized notebook, Field Notes offers compact and durable options that are easy to carry.

Rhodia: Rhodia notebooks come in various sizes and are known for their high-quality paper and distinctive orange covers.

Paperblanks: If you appreciate unique and artistic covers, Paperblanks offers notebooks with beautiful designs and quality construction.

Midori Traveler's Notebook: This modular notebook system allows you to customize and add different inserts for various purposes, making it versatile for musical composition.

You can find these notebooks at various retailers, including stationery stores, bookstores, and online marketplaces. Websites like Amazon, JetPens, and Goulet Pens often carry a wide selection of quality notebooks.

Remember that the best notebook is the one that suits your preferences and enhances your creative process. It's worth exploring different options to find the one that feels right for you.

Sketchbook

If visual elements inspire you, consider using a sketchbook. This allows you to combine written notes with drawings, sketches, or visual representations of your musical ideas.

When choosing a dedicated sketchbook for planning guitar compositions in a musical diary, factors like paper quality, size, and the specific needs of sketching musical ideas become crucial.

Here are some considerations when choosing a sketchbook for the creation of your musical diary:

Paper Quality: High-quality paper in a sketchbook is essential for accommodating various drawing tools, such as pencils, pens, and markers. It should prevent bleed-through and provide a smooth surface for musical notations or sketches.

Recommendation: Look for sketchbooks with thicker paper, preferably 100 gsm or more, to handle different mediums and techniques without compromising the page quality.

Size: The size of the sketchbook depends on personal preference and the level of detail you want to include in your musical sketches. Larger sizes may be preferable if you want more space for intricate notations or illustrations.

Recommendation: Consider sizes like 9x12 inches or larger for ample space, especially if you plan on including detailed musical diagrams.

Visual Flexibility: Sketchbooks provide a more visual and creative space. They allow you to incorporate drawings, diagrams, and visual representations of musical ideas.

Artistic Exploration: If you enjoy exploring different artistic elements alongside your musical compositions, a sketchbook offers more freedom for creativity.

Brand Recommendations:

Strathmore: Strathmore offers a range of sketchbooks with various paper types, including heavyweight options suitable for multiple drawing tools.

Canson XL Series: Canson XL sketchbooks are known for their quality and affordability. They come in different sizes and feature heavyweight paper suitable for sketching.

Moleskine Art Collection: Moleskine offers sketchbooks in various sizes, and their larger options provide a generous canvas for detailed musical compositions.

Stillman & Birn Alpha Series: Known for high-quality sketchbooks, Stillman & Birn provides larger sizes suitable for more expansive musical planning.

It's essential to choose a sketchbook that aligns with your artistic and musical preferences. Exploring different brands and sizes will help you find the ideal sketchbook for planning your guitar compositions.

Binder

Create a loose-leaf system with a binder. This way, you can organize your entries into sections, making it easy to flip through and revisit specific themes or ideas.

Creating a loose-leaf system with a binder or folder for organizing your musical diary entries into sections can be an effective way to keep your ideas structured and easily accessible.

Choose a Binder or Folder: Select a binder or folder that is sturdy, durable, and large enough to hold your loose-leaf pages. The binder should have enough capacity for expansion as you add more entries.

Use Loose-Leaf Paper: Loose-leaf paper allows flexibility in organizing and rearranging your musical diary entries. You can add or move pages as needed.

Create Sections: Divide your binder into sections based on themes, projects, or aspects of your guitar compositions. This makes it easy to locate and revisit specific ideas.

Labeling Entries: Clearly label your entries to quickly identify the content. Use a consistent and intuitive labeling system.

Page Protection: To protect your loose-leaf pages from wear and tear, consider using sheet protectors.

Regular Maintenance: Periodically review and organize your binder, adding new entries and reorganizing sections as needed.

Creating a loose-leaf system with a binder allows you to maintain an organized and easily navigable musical diary for your guitar compositions. The key is to choose high-quality and customizable materials that suit your preferences and provide room for creativity and expansion.

Brand Recommendations:

Avery Durable View Binder: Avery offers durable binders in various sizes with customizable covers. They have a clear view front, allowing you to insert a cover sheet for easy labeling.

Case-it Open Tab Binder: This binder has a unique design with open tabs, making it easy to add and remove pages.

Five Star Reinforced Filler Paper: This paper is reinforced with more durable edges, preventing tearing when added or removed from the binder.

Avery Insertable Dividers: These dividers are customizable, allowing you to label each section with a specific theme or project. The insertable tabs make it easy to update or change labels.

DYMO LabelManager 160: This label maker allows you to create custom labels for your entries. It's easy to use and provides clear and professional-looking labels.

AmazonBasics Sheet Protectors: These clear sheet protectors are standard letter size and fit most binders. They help preserve the quality of your pages.

Index Cards

Use index cards for quick, bite-sized entries. Each card can represent a single idea, making it easy to shuffle, rearrange, and categorize your thoughts.

Using index cards for a musical diary in guitar composition is a tactile and flexible approach that allows you to easily rearrange and organize your ideas.

Here are some benefits to using index cards as a musical diary:

Tactile and Visual: The physicality of index cards makes the creative process more tangible.

Flexibility: Easily experiment with different arrangements and structures.

Portability: Take your index cards with you for on-the-go inspiration.

Idea Generation: Start by jotting down individual musical ideas, chord progressions, or lyrical concepts on separate index cards.

Use a different card for each distinct idea, making sure to keep them concise and focused.

Categorization: Sort the index cards into categories or themes. For example, you might have categories like "Chord Progressions," "Melodies," "Lyrics," or any other relevant aspect of your composition.

Color Coding: Consider using different colors for different categories. This visual distinction makes it easier to identify and work with specific aspects of your composition quickly.

Arranging Ideas: Use a flat surface, such as a table or corkboard, to physically arrange the index cards. Experiment with different arrangements to find the flow and structure that works best for your composition.

Transitional Elements: Introduce additional index cards that represent transitional elements between sections or ideas. These could include cards labeled "Bridge," "Transition," or "Build-up," helping you plan the flow of your composition.

Revision and Experimentation: As you play through or imagine your composition, feel free to move and rearrange the index cards to experiment with different structures. This hands-on approach allows for quick and intuitive changes to your musical ideas.

Recording Details: Write specific details on the index cards, such as tempo, key, or instrumentation. This information ensures that your composition's details are readily available as you work through the arrangement.

Progress Tracking: Use index cards as a visual way to track your progress. Move completed sections to a separate area or mark them to see how your composition is taking shape.

Chord Progression Card: Write down a specific chord progression you like on one card.

Lyrics Card: Jot down lyric ideas or themes on another card.

Tempo/Key Card: Note the tempo and key of a particular section on a separate card.

By using index cards, you can create a dynamic and interactive musical diary that helps you visualize and refine your guitar compositions in a hands-on manner.

DIGITAL MUSICAL DIARY

Note-Taking Apps

Utilize note-taking apps on your computer, tablet, or smartphone. Apps offer flexibility in organizing and syncing your thoughts across devices.

Using note-taking apps for creating a musical diary on your computer, tablet, or smartphone offers digital flexibility and easy synchronization across devices.

Here are some benefits to choosing note-taking apps for your musical diary:

Organize by Sections: Create separate notebooks or sections for different aspects of your guitar compositions (chords, lyrics, melody ideas).

Use Multimedia: Attach audio recordings or images to capture melodies or chord progressions visually.

Tagging: Utilize tagging systems to easily categorize and find related notes.

Cloud Synchronization: Ensure that the app synchronizes your notes across all your devices for seamless accessibility.

Cross-Platform Accessibility: Access your musical diary on various devices.

Search and Organization: Quickly find specific notes using search features and organizational tools.

Collaboration: Some apps offer collaborative features, allowing you to work with others on your musical ideas.

Choose an app that aligns with your preferences and integrates well into your workflow. These digital tools can provide a convenient and versatile **platform** for organizing and developing your guitar compositions.

Here is a short list of note-taking apps available at the time of publishing and the platforms they serve:

Microsoft OneNote:
Platform: Windows, Mac, Android, iOS
Features: Organize notes into notebooks and sections.
Support for text, images, and audio recordings.
Cloud synchronization for access across devices.

Evernote:
Platform: Windows, Mac, Android, iOS
Features: Create notebooks and tag notes for organization. Rich text, images, and audio support.
Synchronization across devices with cloud storage.

Apple Notes:
Platform: iOS, macOS
Features: Seamless integration with Apple devices.
Supports text, sketches, images, and audio. Syncs through iCloud.

Google Keep:
Platform: Web, Android, iOS

Features: Simple and intuitive interface. Supports notes, checklists, images, and voice recordings. Synchronizes with Google account.

Simplenote:
Platform: Windows, Mac, Linux, Android, iOS
Features: Minimalistic and easy-to-use. Fast synchronization between devices. Supports text notes with optional tags.

Turtl:
Platform: Windows, Mac, Linux, Android, iOS
Features: Focus on privacy and security. Organize notes with boards and tags. End-to-end encryption for data.

Notion:
Platform: Web, Windows, Mac, Android, iOS
Features: All-in-one workspace for notes, tasks, and databases. Supports multimedia content. Collaborative features for team projects.

Word Processing Software:

If you prefer a more traditional writing environment, use word processing software like Microsoft Word or Google Docs. Create a dedicated document for your musical diary entries.

Using word processing software for a musical diary allows you to document your guitar compositions in a text-based format, providing a structured and organized platform.

Here are some tips and benefits to using word-processing software to create your musical diary:

Create Sections: Use headings or separate documents for different compositions or themes.

Insert Multimedia: Embed audio recordings, images, or **links** to reference recordings.

Formatting: Utilize formatting options for emphasis, hierarchy, and clarity.

Table of Contents: If your compositions span multiple documents, create a table of contents for easy navigation.

Text-Based Structure: Ideal for detailed descriptions, lyrics, or narratives related to your compositions.

Familiar Interface: Most users are already familiar with word processing software.

Versatile Formatting: Rich formatting options for creating organized and visually appealing documents.

Choose a word processing software based on your preferences, the devices you use, and the level of collaboration required. These tools offer a straightforward and accessible way to maintain a detailed musical diary for your guitar compositions.

Software Recommendations:
Microsoft Word:
Platform: Windows, Mac, Online
Benefits: Familiar and widely used word processing software. Rich formatting options for text, images, and

tables. Easy to create sections or chapters for different compositions.

Google Docs:
Platform: Web, Android, iOS
Benefits: Real-time collaboration with others. Cloud-based storage and easy access from any device. Supports text, images, and links.

Apple Pages:
Platform: Mac, iOS (Available for free on Apple devices)
Benefits: Seamless integration with Apple devices. Rich formatting options for text and multimedia. iCloud synchronization for access across devices.

LibreOffice Writer:
Platform: Windows, Mac, Linux
Benefits: Free and open-source alternative. Supports various document formats. Rich formatting options comparable to Microsoft Word.

Scrivener:
Platform: Windows, Mac
Benefits: Designed for long-form writing and organization. Provides a structured environment with sections and notes. Suitable for writers and composers working on complex projects.

WPS Office:
Platform: Windows, Mac, Linux, Android, iOS

Benefits: Free and feature-rich office suite. Supports a variety of document formats. Cloud synchronization for collaboration and access on different devices.

Choose a word processing software based on your preferences, the devices you use, and the level of collaboration required. These tools offer a straightforward and accessible way to maintain a detailed musical diary for your guitar compositions.

Digital Journal Apps

Explore specialized journaling apps that allow for both text and multimedia entries. Specialized journaling apps can offer a tailored experience for creating a musical diary for guitar compositions.

Here are some tips and benefits to choosing digital journal apps to create your musical diary:

Text-Based Structure: Ideal for detailed descriptions, lyrics, or narratives related to your compositions.

Familiar Interface: Most users are already familiar with word processing software.

Versatile Formatting: Rich formatting options for creating organized and visually appealing documents.

Create Sections: Use headings or separate documents for different compositions or themes.

Insert Multimedia: Embed audio recordings, images, or **links** to reference recordings.

Formatting: Utilize formatting options for emphasis, hierarchy, and clarity.

Table of Contents: If your compositions span multiple documents, create a table of contents for easy navigation.

Multimedia Integration: Take advantage of the ability to include audio recordings, images, and **link**s related to your guitar compositions.

Organization: Use tags, categories, or folders to keep your musical diary entries organized.

Synchronization: Ensure the app syncs seamlessly across your devices to maintain a consistent experience.

Choose a specialized journaling app based on your preferences, the features that align with your needs, and the platforms you use regularly. These apps provide a multimedia-rich environment for documenting and organizing your musical ideas effectively.

Digital Journal App Recommendations:

Day One:
Platform: macOS, iOS, iPadOS, Android
Benefits: Supports text, photos, audio recordings, and tags. Elegant design with a focus on personal journaling. Syncs seamlessly across Apple devices.

Journey:
Platform: Windows, Mac, Android, iOS, ChromeOS, Linux
Benefits: Integrates with Google Drive for cross-**platform** synchronization. Supports multimedia entries

including images and audio recordings. Offers a clean and user-friendly interface.

Penzu:
Platform: Web, iOS, Android
Benefits: Emphasizes privacy with strong encryption. Supports multimedia entries and allows customization. Accessible from any device with a web browser.

Diaro:
Platform: Android, iOS
Benefits: Simple and intuitive interface. Allows multimedia entries and supports tags. Offers an encrypted cloud sync option.

Notion:
Platform: Web, Windows, Mac, Android, iOS
Benefits: Versatile all-in-one workspace with databases, tables, and multimedia support. Ideal for collaborative projects with team members. Available on multiple **platform**s.

Turtl:
Platform: Windows, Mac, Linux, Android, iOS
Benefits: Focuses on privacy and secure data storage. Supports text, images, and file attachments. End-to-end encryption for added security.

Evernote:
Platform: Windows, Mac, Android, iOS

Benefits: Offers a comprehensive set of features for note-taking, including multimedia support. Supports real-time collaboration and synchronization across devices. Integrates well with other apps and services.

Zoho Notebook:
Platform: Web, Windows, Mac, Android, iOS
Benefits: Provides a visually appealing interface with multimedia support. Organize notes in customizable notebooks. Allows collaboration and synchronization across devices.

Online Platforms

Consider creating a blog or using an online platform to document your musical journey. This could be a private blog or a platform like Medium where you share your thoughts and progress with a community.

Creating a blog or using an online platform is an excellent way to document your musical journey and maintain a musical diary for guitar compositions. Blogs provide a public or private space to share your progress, ideas, and reflections.

Here are some benefits and tips to choosing either a private or community-based blogging platform for your musical diary:

Regular Updates: Post regularly to keep your audience or yourself engaged with your musical journey.

Multimedia Integration: Embed audio recordings, videos, or images to enhance your posts.

Tags and Categories: Use tags and categories to organize your content and make it easily searchable.

Interaction: Engage with your audience by responding to comments and participating in the **platform**'s community features.

Privacy Settings: Adjust privacy settings based on whether you want your blog to be public, private, or shared with a specific audience.

Consistency: Maintain a consistent theme or style across your posts for a cohesive and professional-looking blog.

Community Engagement: Community-based **platform**s allow you to connect with other musicians and creators who share similar interests.

Visibility: Public blogs provide a **platform** for sharing your musical journey with a wider audience, gaining feedback, and potentially connecting with collaborators.

Organization: Blogs offer a structured way to chronicle your musical experiences, compositions, and progress over time.

Whether you choose a private blog for personal reflection or a community-based platform for broader engagement, blogging can be a powerful tool to document your musical journey and compositions.

Here are examples of both private blog platforms and community-based blogging platforms:

Private Blog Platforms:

WordPress.com:
Benefits: Offers both free and premium plans. Provides various themes and customization options. Can be set as private or public.

Medium:
Benefits: Simple and minimalist design. Can be set to private or shared with a select audience. Focuses on content and storytelling.

Community-Based Blogging Platforms:
Tumblr:
Benefits: Emphasizes short-form content, suitable for quick updates. Offers a social component with a reblogging system. Allows a mix of multimedia content.

Blogger:
Benefits: Owned by Google, making integration with other services seamless. Simple interface for quick blogging. Supports multimedia content.

Steemit:
Benefits: Operates on blockchain technology, rewarding users for engagement. Content can be monetized through cryptocurrency. Integrates a community-driven voting system.

Voice Recorder Apps

Use voice recorder apps on your smartphone to capture spoken ideas, hummed melodies, or verbal reflections. Later, you can transcribe or integrate these recordings into your digital diary.

Using voice recorder apps to create a musical diary for guitar compositions can be a convenient and efficient method to capture ideas on the go.

Convenience and Spontaneity: Voice recorder apps allow you to capture musical ideas wherever inspiration strikes, whether you're playing your guitar at home, walking outside, or commuting.

Capture Melodies and Chord Progressions: You can easily hum melodies, strum chord progressions, or sing lyric ideas into the recorder, preserving the raw essence of your musical thoughts.

Quick Reference for Later: Voice recordings serve as a quick reference for recalling specific sounds, tones, or rhythms, making it easier to recreate your ideas during the composition process.

Capture Lyric Ideas: For songwriters, voice recorder apps are great for capturing lyric ideas, vocal melodies, or spoken-word thoughts that may be part of the overall composition.

Multi-Device Accessibility: Many voice recorder apps offer cloud synchronization, allowing you to access your recordings across multiple devices and seamlessly integrate them into your digital workflow.

Auditory Feedback: Listening back to your recordings provides immediate auditory feedback, allowing you to evaluate and refine your musical ideas with a fresh perspective.

Integration with Other Apps: Some voice recorder apps integrate with other music creation apps or software, making it easy to import your recorded ideas into your digital audio workstation (DAW) for further development.

Organize Recordings: Use labels, tags, or folders within the app to organize your recordings by theme, project, or date.

Regular Backups: Ensure your recordings are regularly backed up to prevent accidental loss.

Experimentation: Use the voice recorder app for experimentation and exploration, capturing both planned and spontaneous musical ideas.

Voice recorder apps provide a versatile and accessible tool for documenting your musical ideas, allowing you to effortlessly capture, organize, and revisit your guitar compositions.

Music Notation Software

If you prefer a more structured approach, use music notation software like Finale or MuseScore to document musical ideas. Create a digital score for your composition, adding annotations about inspirations and emotions.

Music notation software is a powerful tool for creating and organizing a musical diary for guitar compositions. These applications allow you to notate your musical ideas, create sheet music, and organize your compositions efficiently.

Here are some tips if you decide to create your musical diary using notation software:

Learn the Basics: Familiarize yourself with the basic functions of the software to enhance your efficiency.

Use Guitar Tablature: Take advantage of guitar tablature features to notate specific fingerings and techniques.

Experiment with Playback: Most software allows you to play back your compositions, which can aid in the composition and arrangement process.

Explore Templates: Many software programs provide templates for various genres, including guitar compositions.

Choose a music notation software based on your skill level, preferences, and the specific features you need. These tools can significantly enhance your ability to document and develop your guitar compositions in a systematic and professional manner.

Brand Recommendations:
Sibelius
Platform: Windows, Mac
Benefits: Industry-standard music notation software. Advanced features for professional composers. Support for guitar tablature and traditional notation.

Finale
Platform: Windows, Mac
Benefits: Robust and versatile music notation software. Customizable and suitable for a wide range of music genres. Supports guitar tablature and offers detailed control over notation.

Guitar Pro
Platform: Windows, Mac, Linux, iOS, Android

Benefits: Specifically designed for guitarists and bassists. Features a user-friendly interface. Supports both standard notation and guitar tablature.

Musescore

Platform: Windows, Mac, Linux

Benefits: Free and open-source music notation software. User-friendly interface suitable for beginners. Supports guitar tablature and standard notation.

Notion

Platform: Windows, Mac, iOS, Android

Benefits: All-in-one workspace with notation, audio, and more. User-friendly and intuitive interface. Real-time collaboration for team projects.

Dorico

Platform: Windows, Mac

Benefits: Advanced music notation software with intelligent features. Professional-grade scoring and engraving capabilities. Supports guitar tablature and standard notation.

LilyPond

Platform: Windows, Mac, Linux

Benefits: Free and open-source music engraving software. Text-based input for precise control. Suitable for those comfortable with command-line interfaces.

Flat.io

Platform: Web, iOS, Android

Benefits: Cloud-based music notation platform. Collaborative features for real-time sharing and editing. Supports guitar tablature and standard notation.

APPROACHES AND BEST PRACTICES FOR YOUR MUSICAL DIARY

THE HYBRID APPROACH OF ANALOG AND DIGITAL

Some musicians prefer a hybrid approach, combining both analog and digital tools. For instance, you might use a physical notebook for initial brainstorming and sketches and then transfer key ideas to a digital platform for organization and accessibility.

Setting up a hybrid system for a musical diary that combines analog and digital tools involves strategically integrating both to maximize the benefits of each.

Initial Ideas and Inspiration

Analog Tool: Begin with a physical notebook or sketchbook.

Use the notebook to jot down initial ideas, lyrics, chord progressions, or any spontaneous thoughts that come to mind. Capture sketches or visual representations of your musical concepts.

Digital Tool: Consider using a voice recorder app.

Record voice memos to capture melodies, hummed tunes, or verbal explanations of your ideas.

Voice recordings offer a quick and efficient way to document initial inspiration.

Development and Sketching

Analog Tool: Continue using the physical notebook and sketchbook.

Flesh out your ideas in more detail, including chord diagrams, song structures, and rough sketches of compositions. Annotate your sketches with additional thoughts or considerations.

Digital Tool: Introduce a note-taking app.

Transfer analog sketches or written notes to a digital format using your note-taking app. Add tags or labels to digitally organize and categorize your entries.

Detailed Compositions and Notation

Analog Tool: Use the sketchbook or dedicated sheet music notebook.

Create more detailed compositions, incorporating sheet music elements such as notation, dynamics, and tempo markings. Consider adding detailed annotations or ideas around the notated music.

Digital Tool: Employ music notation software.

Transfer your analog compositions into digital notation software (e.g., Guitar Pro, Sibelius) for precise notation, arrangement, and playback. Save and organize digital compositions for easy retrieval.

Integration and Synchronization

Analog to Digital: Capture photos or scan pages from your physical notebook or sketchbook.

Upload these images to your cloud storage service (e.g., Dropbox, Google Drive) or note-taking app. Tag or categorize the digital entries for better organization.

Digital to Analog: Print out digital compositions or notations.

Integrate printed versions into your physical notebook or sheet music binder.

Collaboration and Feedback

Analog Tool: Share printed versions with collaborators or fellow musicians for feedback.

Gather handwritten annotations and suggestions on the printed copies.

Digital Tool: Leverage collaborative features of note-taking apps or cloud storage.

Share digital entries with collaborators, allowing for real-time comments and edits. Use the digital versions for collaborative discussions and remote feedback.

Revision and Refinement

Analog Tool: Use the physical notebook for ongoing revision and refinement.

Make additional notes, corrections, or modifications directly in the notebook.

Digital Tool: Continue using note-taking apps or music notation software.

Update digital entries based on revisions made in the physical notebook. Ensure that both analog and digital versions stay synchronized.

Finalizing and Archiving

Analog Tool: Consider using a dedicated binder for finalized compositions.

Arrange printed compositions in a chronological or thematic order. Create sections for different projects or phases.

Digital Tool: Keep your digital entries organized within the note-taking app or cloud storage.

Archive completed projects or compositions. Maintain a well-organized digital library for easy access.

Regular Review and Reflection

Analog Tool: Flip through the physical notebook periodically.

Reflect on the journey by reviewing initial ideas and the evolution of your compositions.

Digital Tool: Use the note-taking app or cloud storage analytics.

Utilize the search and analytics features to identify patterns or recurring themes across your musical diary.

By seamlessly integrating analog and digital tools at each stage, you create a comprehensive hybrid system that caters to the strengths of both approaches. This allows for a flexible and dynamic musical diary for your guitar compositions.

SCANNING OR PHOTOGRAPHING PHYSICAL ENTRIES

If you choose analog tools but want the benefits of digital organization, consider scanning or photographing your physical entries. This allows you to create a digital archive while maintaining the tactile experience of a physical diary.

If you choose analog tools for your musical diary and want to create a digital archive of each entry, there are several methods and tools you can employ to bridge the gap between analog and digital.

Digital Scanning

Use a scanner or smartphone with scanning capabilities to create digital copies of your analog entries. Save the scanned images as digital files.

Tools:

Scanner: If you have access to a flatbed scanner, it provides high-quality scans.

Smartphone Apps: Apps like Adobe Scan, Microsoft Office Lens, or Google Drive can be used for quick scanning using your phone's camera.

Photography

Take high-quality photographs of your analog entries using a digital camera or smartphone. Ensure good lighting and focus for clarity.

Tools:

Digital Camera: A dedicated digital camera provides high-resolution images.

Smartphone Camera: Modern smartphones often have powerful cameras suitable for capturing detailed images.

Note-Taking Apps with Image Upload

Use note-taking apps that support image uploads. Upload the scanned or photographed images of your analog entries to these apps.

Tools:

Evernote: Allows you to create digital notebooks and upload images.

OneNote: Microsoft's note-taking app that supports image insertion.

Notion: An all-in-one workspace where you can organize textual and visual content.

Cloud Storage

Upload your digital images to cloud storage services for safekeeping and accessibility. Organize the files into folders based on themes, projects, or dates.

Tools:

Dropbox: A cloud storage service that syncs files across devices.

Google Drive: Google's cloud storage solution with seamless integration into other Google services.

Microsoft OneDrive: Offers cloud storage and synchronization, particularly suitable for Windows users.

Digital Notebooks

Use digital notebook applications that support image uploads and annotations. Import digital images of your analog entries into these digital notebooks.

Tools:

GoodNotes (iPad): An app that allows you to import images, annotate, and organize them digitally.

Notability (iPad): Similar to GoodNotes, offering features for importing and annotating images.

Blogging Platforms

Create a private blog where you can upload images and document your musical journey. Write accompanying text for each entry to provide context.

Tools:

WordPress.com: Offers a private blog option.

Medium: Allows you to create private stories or articles.

Digital Scrapbooking Apps

Utilize digital scrapbooking apps designed for preserving memories with images and text. Create digital collages of your analog entries.

Tools:

Project Life (App): Designed for digital scrapbooking and memory keeping.

Canva (Web/ App): A versatile graphic design tool suitable for creating visual collages.

Tips for Creating a Digital Archive

Consistent Naming: Use a consistent naming convention for your digital files to make them easily searchable.

Metadata: Add metadata or tags to your digital files for better organization.

Regular Backups: Ensure that your digital archive is regularly backed up to prevent data loss.

By employing these methods and tools, you can seamlessly create a digital archive of your analog musical diary, preserving your handwritten or sketched entries in a digital format for easy access, sharing, and long-term storage.

Choose the method or combination of methods that best suits your workflow and preferences. The goal is to create a tool that enhances your creative process, making it easy to capture and revisit the ideas and inspirations that contribute to your guitar composition.

CLOUD STORAGE

Store your digital diary in cloud storage services like Dropbox or Google Drive. This ensures that your entries are accessible from multiple devices and are backed up securely.

Using cloud storage to store your musical diary for guitar composition offers the advantage of accessibility, collaboration, and data security.

Here are some benefits to utilizing cloud storage for your musical diary:

Organize Folders: Create specific folders for different aspects of your guitar compositions, such as lyrics, chord progressions, and audio recordings.

Collaborate: Leverage collaboration features to work with other musicians or collaborators.

Regular Backups: Ensure that your musical diary is regularly backed up to prevent data loss.

Using cloud storage provides a centralized and secure location for storing your musical diary, allowing you to access your compositions from various devices and collaborate with others seamlessly. Choose a **platform** based on your storage needs, collaboration requirements, and device compatibility.

Some popular cloud storage platforms include:

Google Drive:
Benefits: Offers 15 GB of free storage. Seamless integration with other Google services. Real-time collaboration on documents. Accessible on the web, Windows, Mac, Android, and iOS.

Dropbox:
Benefits: Provides 2 GB of free storage with options to earn more through referrals. Easy file sharing and collaboration. Compatible with various devices and operating systems. Integration with third-party apps.

Microsoft OneDrive:
Benefits: Comes with 5 GB of free storage. Integrated with Microsoft Office apps. Real-time collaboration on documents. Accessible on the web, Windows, Mac, Android, and iOS.

iCloud:
Benefits: Offers 5 GB of free storage. Seamless integration with Apple devices and services. Automatic

backups for iOS devices. Accessible on the web, macOS, iOS, and Windows.

Box:

Benefits: Provides 10 GB of free storage with file size limitations. Strong security features with advanced collaboration tools. Integration with third-party apps. Accessible on the web, Windows, Mac, Android, and iOS.

Amazon Drive:

Benefits: Offers 5 GB of free storage with additional storage available for purchase. Prime members receive unlimited photo storage. Integration with Amazon services. Accessible on the web, Windows, Mac, Android, and iOS.

pCloud:

Benefits: Provides 10 GB of free storage with opportunities to earn more through referrals. Focus on user-friendly features and file sharing. Cross-**platform** compatibility. Client-side encryption for added security.

Sync.com:

Benefits: Offers 5 GB of free storage with client-side encryption. Emphasis on privacy and security. Easy file sharing and collaboration. Cross-**platform** compatibility.

YOUR MUSICAL DIARY ENTRIES

SET A REGULAR WRITING SCHEDULE

Establish a consistent schedule for writing in your musical diary. Whether it's daily, weekly, or as ideas strike, having a routine helps capture a broad range of thoughts and experiences.

Establishing a regular writing schedule for your musical diary is essential for maintaining consistency and capturing the evolution of your creative process over time.

A regular writing schedule will enhance your creativity, organization, and overall musical development.

To set clear goals for this endeavor, consider the following tips and examples:

Set Clear Goals

Define the goals you want to achieve through your musical diary. Whether it's documenting inspirations, refining ideas, or tracking your emotional journey, clear goals provide direction for your writing.

Define Your Purpose

Tip: Clarify why you want to maintain a regular writing schedule. Is it to document your creative process, track progress, or gather inspiration for future compositions?

Example Goal: *"Establish a consistent writing schedule to document my daily musical thoughts, explore new ideas, and track the evolution of my compositions."*

Set Realistic Frequency

Tip: Be realistic about how often you can commit to writing in your musical diary. Consider your current schedule, commitments, and energy levels.

Example Goal: *"Write in my musical diary at least three times a week, allocating dedicated time during my most productive hours."*

Designate Specific Time Slots

Tip: Schedule specific time slots for your musical diary sessions. Consistency helps form a habit, and designated slots prevent procrastination.

Example Goal: *"Write in my musical diary every Monday, Wednesday, and Friday from 7:00 PM to 8:00 PM."*

Set Clear Objectives

Tip: Clearly define what you aim to achieve during each writing session. It could be brainstorming new melodies, refining chord progressions, or documenting lyrical ideas.

Example Goal: *"During each session, focus on either refining an existing composition, experimenting with new chord progressions, or documenting lyrical ideas."*

Experiment with Formats

Tip: Try different formats within your writing sessions, such as freeform journaling, structured outlines, or specific prompts. This keeps your writing dynamic and prevents monotony.

Example Goal: *"Experiment with different formats throughout the month, dedicating one week to freeform journaling, the next to structured outlines, and the following to exploring specific prompts."*

Track Progress and Reflect

Tip: Include a goal to regularly review and reflect on your entries. This helps you gauge progress, identify patterns, and gain insights into your creative process.

Example Goal: *"At the end of each month, review my musical diary entries to track progress, identify recurring themes, and reflect on areas for improvement or exploration."*

Incorporate Inspiration Sources

Tip: Integrate sources of inspiration into your writing schedule. This could include listening to new music, attending live performances, or exploring other artistic mediums.

Example Goal: *"Once a week, dedicate a portion of my writing session to exploring new music genres, attending virtual concerts, or drawing inspiration from other art forms."*

Celebrate Milestones

Tip: Set milestones for your musical diary and celebrate achievements. This could be completing a certain number of entries, achieving consistency for a month, or successfully experimenting with a new composition technique.

Example Goal: *"Celebrate achieving a consistent writing schedule for three consecutive months by treating myself to a special musical experience or reward."*

Stay Adaptable

Tip: Life can be unpredictable, so build flexibility into your schedule. Be open to adjusting your writing routine if unexpected commitments arise.

Example Goal: *"Adapt my writing schedule when necessary, but aim to make up missed sessions within the same week to maintain consistency."*

Accountability and Sharing

Tip: Share your goals with a friend, mentor, or fellow musician. Having someone to hold you accountable can provide motivation and encouragement.

Example Goal: *"Share my commitment to a regular writing schedule with a fellow musician, and schedule periodic check-ins to discuss progress, challenges, and successes."*

By setting clear and achievable goals for your regular writing schedule, you can develop a consistent and meaningful practice that contributes to your growth as a guitarist and composer. Adjust your goals over time to align with your evolving needs and aspirations in your musical journey.

IDENTIFY IDEAL FREQUENCY

Determine how often you want to make entries in your musical diary. Consider your schedule, commitments, and the pace of your creative process. Aim for a frequency that is sustainable for you, whether it's daily, weekly, or another interval.

Identifying the ideal frequency for making a sustainable entry schedule in your musical diary for guitar composition involves finding a balance that suits your lifestyle, creativity, and overall goals.

Consider Your Schedule

Tip: Evaluate your daily and weekly schedule to identify pockets of time where you can consistently dedicate yourself to musical diary entries.

Example: If you have more free time on weekends, consider scheduling longer and more in-depth entries during those days.

Start Small and Gradually Increase

Tip: Begin with a manageable frequency, and gradually increase it as you build the habit. Starting small helps prevent burnout.

Example: Start by committing to two entries per week. Once this becomes a routine, consider increasing it to three or four entries.

Align with Your Energy Levels

Tip: Schedule your entries during times when you feel most energized and creative. This ensures that your entries are more meaningful and enjoyable.

Example: If you are a morning person, consider making your entries during the early hours when your mind is fresh.

Quality Over Quantity

Tip: Prioritize the quality of your entries over the quantity. Focus on meaningful reflections, ideas, and compositions rather than trying to meet a specific entry count.

Example: Aim for two well-thought-out and detailed entries per week rather than five rushed and superficial ones.

Be Realistic About Commitments

Tip: Assess your current commitments, including work, family, and other responsibilities. Choose a frequency that is realistic and doesn't conflict with your existing obligations.

Example: If you have a busy workweek, opt for a lower frequency and dedicate more time on weekends.

Experiment with Different Frequencies

Tip: Be open to experimenting with different entry frequencies to find what works best for you. You might discover that a specific frequency enhances your creativity and consistency.

Example: Try writing in your musical diary three times a week for a month, then switch to a daily schedule for the following month to compare the impact on your musical output.

Set Monthly Goals

Tip: Instead of focusing on a fixed weekly schedule, set monthly entry goals. This approach provides more flexibility and allows you to adapt based on your monthly calendar.

Example: Aim to complete 12 meaningful entries per month, allowing you to distribute your efforts based on weekly variations.

Prioritize Self-Care

Tip: Consider your overall well-being when setting your entry frequency. Ensure that your schedule allows for adequate rest and self-care to prevent burnout.

Example: If you have a particularly demanding period, be flexible with your schedule and prioritize rest when needed.

Adjust Based on Feedback

Tip: Pay attention to how your creative process evolves with your chosen frequency. If you find yourself consistently inspired or struggling, be willing to adjust your schedule accordingly.

Example: If you feel invigorated and inspired, consider adding an extra entry each week. Conversely, if you're feeling overwhelmed, scale back temporarily.

Celebrate Consistency

Tip: Celebrate the consistency of your entries rather than adhering strictly to a set frequency. Acknowledge your achievements and progress, even if the frequency varies at times.

Example: Celebrate reaching your entry goal for the month with a small reward or by sharing your accomplishments with fellow musicians.

By considering these tips and tailoring them to your personal circumstances, you can identify the ideal frequency for making a sustainable entry schedule in your musical diary. This approach will help you cultivate meaningful entries and contribute to the development of your guitar compositions over time.

ALLOCATE SPECIFIC TIME

Allocate a specific time in your day dedicated to writing in your musical diary. This could be in the morning, during lunch, or before bedtime. Having a designated time helps establish a routine.

The time of day when you write in your musical diary for guitar composition can significantly impact your creativity, focus, and overall productivity.

Here are some pros and cons associated with different times of the day, along with tips and examples:

Morning

Pros:

Fresh Mind: Mornings often bring a fresh and rested mind, making it an ideal time for creative thinking.

Quiet Atmosphere: The morning can be quieter, providing a conducive environment for deep concentration.

Cons:

Warming Up: It might take some time to fully wake up and get into a creative flow.

Time Constraints: If you have a busy morning schedule, finding extended periods for creative work might be challenging.

Tips: Begin your day a bit earlier to have dedicated time for your musical diary before other commitments.

Afternoon

Pros

Increased Energy: Energy levels tend to rise in the afternoon, making it easier to stay focused.

Warmed Up: By this time, your mind is usually warmed up, reducing the need for an extended warm-up period.

Cons

Potential Distractions: Afternoons can be busier with external commitments or interruptions.

Post-Lunch Slump: Some people experience a post-lunch energy dip, affecting creativity.

Tips: Plan your writing sessions around your schedule, taking advantage of breaks or quieter periods.

Evening

Pros

Reflective Atmosphere: Evenings can offer a reflective and relaxed atmosphere, conducive to introspective composition.

Day's Experiences: Drawing from the day's experiences and emotions can inspire creative expressions.

Cons

Fatigue: By evening, you may experience mental fatigue from the day's activities.

Distractions: Family or social obligations can create interruptions during evening sessions.

Tips: Take some time to unwind before your session to transition from the day's activities.

Night

Pros

Quiet Atmosphere: Nights are often quiet, providing a serene environment for focused creativity.

No Time Constraints: Depending on your schedule, you may have more time at night without external interruptions.

Cons

Potential Fatigue: If you've had a long day, mental fatigue may impact the quality of your compositions.

Sleep Schedule: Late-night sessions might interfere with your sleep schedule.

Tips: Focus on quality rather than quantity, especially if it's late and you're feeling tired.

TIPS FOR CHOOSING THE RIGHT TIME

Experiment

Example: Try different times of the day for a week each and evaluate your productivity and creativity during those periods.

Align with Natural Rhythms

Example: If you're a morning person, prioritize morning sessions. If you're a night owl, consider nighttime for your creative endeavors.

Combine Schedules

Example: If mornings are ideal for creative thinking but evenings are more relaxed, consider a two-part schedule: brainstorming in the morning and refining in the evening.

Observe Energy Peaks

Example: Pay attention to your natural energy peaks and lows throughout the day. Plan your writing sessions during high-energy periods.

Consistency Matters

Example: While flexibility is essential, consistency in your chosen time can help establish a routine that aligns with your body's natural rhythms.

Ultimately, the best time for writing in your musical diary depends on your personal preferences, lifestyle, and daily schedule. Experimenting with different times and observing your own patterns will help you identify the most productive and creative periods for your guitar composition entries.

CREATE A RITUAL

Develop a ritual or routine that signals the beginning of your writing session. It could be making a cup of tea, listening to a favorite song, or simply taking a few moments of quiet reflection.

Creating a ritual to signal the beginning of your writing session in your musical diary for guitar composition can help set the mood, enhance focus, and create a conducive environment for creativity.

Designate a Dedicated Space

Tip: Choose a specific location for your writing sessions. This could be a cozy corner, a particular room, or even an outdoor space.

Example: Set up a comfortable chair and a small table in a corner of your room where you can keep your musical instruments, notebooks, and any other tools you use for composition.

Select Inspirational Music

Tip: Create a playlist of music that inspires you or complements the mood you want to set for your composition session.

Example: Before starting your writing session, listen to a few tracks that resonate with the style or emotions you want to explore in your composition.

Mindful Breathing Exercise

Tip: Begin your session with a brief mindful breathing exercise to center your mind and promote focus.

Example: Take five minutes to sit quietly, close your eyes, and focus on your breath. Inhale deeply, exhale slowly, and clear your mind of distractions.

Set a Clear Intention

Tip: Before you start writing, set a clear intention for your session. What do you want to achieve or explore?

Example: Verbally or mentally express your intention, such as "I am open to new melodies and innovative chord progressions."

Warm-Up Exercises

Tip: Include warm-up exercises to get your fingers moving and your mind engaged in the creative process.

Example: Play through scales, practice fingerpicking, or perform any technique exercises relevant to your musical goals for the session.

Visual Cues

Tip: Use visual cues to signal the start of your writing session. This could be a specific object, a piece of artwork, or even a lit candle.

Example: Light a candle as a symbolic representation of igniting your creative spark, signaling the beginning of your composition time.

Journaling Warm-Up

Tip: Begin your session with a brief journaling warm-up where you jot down any thoughts, feelings, or ideas that come to mind.

Example: Write a stream of consciousness for five minutes to clear your mind and pave the way for focused composition.

Create a Signature Drink or Snack

Tip: Prepare a signature drink or snack that you consume only during your writing sessions. This can create a sensory association with creativity.

Example: Make a special cup of tea or coffee, or have a small bowl of nuts or fruits reserved for your composition sessions.

Digital Detox

Tip: Consider a brief digital detox before your writing session to minimize distractions and enhance focus.

Example: Turn off notifications on your phone, close unnecessary tabs on your computer, and create a dedicated, distraction-free environment.

Review Previous Entries

Tip: Begin your session by reviewing your previous entries. This can provide continuity and help you build on existing ideas.

Example: Spend a few minutes revisiting your last entry, reflecting on any unresolved ideas or themes you want to explore further.

Express Gratitude

Tip: Start your session with a moment of gratitude. Reflect on what you appreciate in your musical journey.

Example: Take a moment to express gratitude for the opportunity to create music and explore your artistic expression through your guitar compositions.

Sensory Environment

Tip: Consider incorporating sensory elements into your ritual, such as lighting a scented candle or having a specific texture (like a soft blanket) for added comfort.

Example: Light a lavender-scented candle or wrap yourself in a cozy blanket to engage your senses and create a comfortable space for creativity.

Tips for Building Effective Rituals

Personalize: Tailor your rituals to suit your preferences and preferences.

Consistency: Aim for consistency to establish a routine that signals the start of your creative sessions.

Evolve Over Time: Be open to adjusting and evolving your rituals as your creative process and needs change.

By incorporating a ritual into your writing sessions, you create a structured and intentional environment that supports your guitar composition journey. Experiment with different elements until you find a combination that resonates with you and enhances your creative flow.

ELIMINATE DISTRACTIONS

Minimize distractions during your writing time. Turn off notifications, choose a quiet environment, and inform others around you about your dedicated writing period.

Distractions can hinder the creative process when writing in your musical diary for guitar composition.

Designate a Dedicated Space

Tip: Choose a specific space for your writing sessions that is free from common distractions.

Example: Set up a comfortable and quiet corner in your home where you can focus on your guitar compositions without interruptions.

Establish a Clear Schedule

Tip: Set specific time slots for your musical diary entries to create a routine. Communicate your schedule to others to minimize disruptions.

Example: Designate 7:00 PM to 8:00 PM every day as your dedicated writing time, ensuring that others are aware of your commitment during those hours.

Prioritize Tasks

Tip: Tackle important tasks and potential distractions before your writing session to clear your mind.

Example: If household chores or work-related responsibilities could distract you, address them beforehand to create a focused and clutter-free mental space.

Set Boundaries with Others

Tip: Communicate your need for uninterrupted time with family or housemates and establish clear boundaries.

Example: Let others know that you'll be working on your musical diary and need focused time, minimizing the likelihood of interruptions.

Use Noise-Canceling Headphones

Tip: Invest in noise-canceling headphones to block out ambient sounds and create a focused auditory environment.

Example: Wear noise-canceling headphones to eliminate background noise and immerse yourself in your guitar compositions.

Create a To-Do List

Tip: Before starting your session, create a to-do list to organize your thoughts and prioritize tasks. This can help reduce mental clutter.

Example: Jot down specific goals for your writing session, such as refining a chord progression or exploring new lyrical ideas.

Limit Access to Gadgets

Tip: If possible, limit access to distracting gadgets or move them out of reach during your writing sessions.

Example: Place your phone in another room or use apps that lock your device for a set period to prevent impulsive distractions.

Batch Process Communication

Tip: Set specific times for communication, such as checking emails or messages, to avoid constant interruptions.

Example: Allocate 15 minutes at the beginning and end of your writing session to respond to emails or messages, minimizing disruptions.

Establish Accountability

Tip: Share your commitment to focused writing sessions with a friend or family member who can help hold you accountable.

Example: Inform a trusted friend about your writing goals, and ask them to check in on your progress regularly, providing an external layer of accountability.

Reflect on Distractions

Tip: If distractions persist, take a moment to reflect on their source. Identify patterns and find proactive solutions to address recurring distractions.

Example: If certain types of notifications consistently disrupt your sessions, adjust your device settings or use apps designed to minimize interruptions.

Reward System

Tip: Establish a reward system for maintaining focus during your writing sessions. This can serve as positive reinforcement.

Example: Treat yourself to a small reward, like a favorite snack or short break, after successfully completing a distraction-free writing session.

By implementing these tips and examples, you can create an environment that minimizes distractions and supports your concentration during guitar composition sessions in your musical diary. Tailor these strategies to your preferences and adjust as needed to enhance the effectiveness of your writing routine.

START SMALL

If you're new to maintaining a writing schedule, start with a manageable duration. You can gradually increase the time as you become more accustomed to the routine.

Starting small and gradually increasing the duration of your writing sessions in your musical diary for guitar composition is a effective way to build a sustainable and enjoyable writing habit.

Set Realistic Goals

Tip: Start with a realistic and achievable goal for your initial writing sessions. This could be as short as 10-15 minutes.

Example: Begin by committing to writing in your musical diary for just 10 minutes every day. This makes the task feel manageable and less overwhelming.

Consistency is Key

Tip: Focus on consistency rather than the duration initially. Aim to write in your musical diary every day or on specific days of the week.

Example: Commit to writing for 10 minutes every day for the next week. Consistency will help establish the habit.

Focus on One Aspect

Tip: Instead of trying to compose an entire piece, focus on one specific aspect of your composition during shorter sessions.

Example: Dedicate a 10-minute session to experimenting with different chord progressions or refining a specific section of a song.

Use Prompts

Tip: Use prompts or writing exercises to jumpstart your creativity during shorter sessions.

Example: Set a timer for 10 minutes and write down as many lyrical ideas as you can based on a given prompt, like "nostalgia" or "adventure."

Reflect and Plan

Tip: Spend a few minutes at the end of each short session reflecting on what you achieved and planning for the next session.

Example: After a 10-minute writing session, jot down any insights, ideas, or tasks to explore in future, longer sessions.

Gradually Increase Duration

Tip: Once you feel comfortable with the shorter durations, gradually increase the time spent on your musical diary entries.

Example: After a week of 10-minute sessions, extend your writing time to 15 minutes for the next week.

Celebrate Small Achievements

Tip: Acknowledge and celebrate small achievements to reinforce the positive habit.

Example: Treat yourself to a small reward or a brief break after completing a week of consistent 10-minute writing sessions.

Monitor Your Progress

Tip: Keep track of your progress by noting the duration and content of each session. This helps you visualize your growth.

Example: Maintain a log or calendar where you record the duration and key highlights of each writing session.

Listen to Your Energy Levels

Tip: Pay attention to your energy levels during writing sessions. If you find your focus waning, consider taking a short break and returning later.

Example: If you feel fatigued after 10 minutes, take a 5-minute break before resuming or extend the break between sessions.

Experiment with Session Timing

Tip: Experiment with different times of the day to find when you are most alert and creative.

Example: If mornings are more conducive to focus, consider extending your sessions gradually during that time.

Make it Enjoyable

Tip: Ensure that your writing sessions remain enjoyable and fulfilling, even as you increase their duration.

Example: Incorporate elements you love, such as playing your favorite tunes or exploring genres that inspire you, to maintain enthusiasm.

Build Incrementally

Tip: Incrementally increase the duration based on your comfort level. Aim for gradual progress rather than sudden, drastic changes.

Example: If you started with 10-minute sessions, increase it to 20 minutes once you feel ready, then continue progressing at a pace that suits you.

Stay Patient

Tip: Building a habit takes time, so be patient with yourself. Consistency is more important than the length of each individual session.

Example: If you miss a day or need to shorten a session, acknowledge it and commit to returning to your routine the next day.

By starting small and gradually increasing the duration of your writing sessions, you create a sustainable and adaptable practice that aligns with your natural rhythm and lifestyle. This approach allows you to cultivate a meaningful musical diary for guitar composition while enjoying the creative process.

USE REMINDERS OR ALARMS

Set reminders or alarms to prompt your writing sessions. This helps reinforce the habit until it becomes ingrained in your daily or weekly routine.

To prompt your writing sessions in your musical diary for guitar composition, you can utilize various reminders and alarms available through different platforms and devices.

Smartphone Alarms

Tip: Set daily or weekly alarms on your smartphone to remind you of your designated writing time.

Example: Use the built-in clock or alarm app on your smartphone to create recurring reminders for your preferred writing schedule.

Calendar App Reminders

Tip: Utilize calendar apps to schedule and receive notifications for your writing sessions.

Example: Use Google Calendar, Apple Calendar, or any preferred calendar app to set up recurring events with reminders for your writing sessions.

Task Management Apps

Tip: Incorporate task management apps that allow you to create to-do lists with reminders for your writing sessions.

Example: Apps like Todoist or Microsoft To Do, let you set tasks with reminders for your musical diary entries.

Digital Voice Assistants

Tip: If you have a smart speaker or digital voice assistant, use voice commands to set up reminders.

Example: Tell devices like Amazon Echo or Google Home, *"Set a daily reminder for my musical diary at 7:00 PM."*

Wearable Devices

Tip: If you wear a smartwatch or fitness tracker, leverage the reminder features on these devices.

Example: Set up reminders using the alarm or reminder functions on devices like Apple Watch, Fitbit, or Garmin.

Email Reminders

Tip: Schedule email reminders to prompt your writing sessions, especially if you regularly check your email.

Example: Use the built-in email reminder feature or third-party tools that integrate with your email client.

Desktop Notifications

Tip: If you spend a significant amount of time on your computer, use desktop notifications to remind you of writing sessions.

Example: Tools like Microsoft Outlook, Google Calendar, or browser extensions can provide desktop notifications for your scheduled sessions.

Specialized Writing Apps

Tip: Consider using writing or journaling apps that include built-in reminders for your musical diary entries.

Example: Apps like Day One, Journey, or Penzu often have reminder features to prompt your writing sessions.

Custom Alarms on Musical Instruments

Tip: Set alarms or reminders directly on your musical instruments if they have built-in features.

Example: Some digital keyboards or electronic guitars allow you to set reminders or alarms using their onboard settings.

Combination of Multiple Reminders

Tip: Combine various reminder methods for increased effectiveness. For instance, use a smartphone alarm along with a calendar reminder.

Example: Set an alarm on your phone for 5 minutes before your scheduled writing session, and have a calendar event with a reminder at the same time.

Location-Based Reminders

Tip: Use location-based reminders if you want prompts when you are in a specific place.

Example: Apps like Apple's Reminders or Google Keep allow you to set location-based reminders for your writing sessions.

IFTTT Automations

Tip: Explore IFTTT (If This Then That) to create custom automations for reminders based on triggers like time or location.

Example: Set up an IFTTT applet that sends you a reminder notification every day at your designated writing time.

Browser Extensions

Tip: If you use web browsers frequently, install browser extensions that provide reminders.

Example: Extensions like "Reminder" for Chrome or "Todoist for Chrome" integrate with your browser to prompt your writing sessions.

Integrated Mobile Apps

Tip: Use integrated mobile apps that combine writing and reminders in one **platform**.

Example: Apps like Evernote or Microsoft OneNote offer both writing capabilities and built-in reminder features.

Personalized Voice Memos

Tip: Record a personalized voice memo on your smartphone or smart speaker to serve as a daily reminder.

Example: Record a message saying, "It's time for your musical diary session," and set it as a daily alarm.

Tips for Effective Reminders

Consistency: Set reminders for the same time each day to establish a consistent writing routine.

Adjust as Needed: Be open to adjusting the timing or method of reminders based on your evolving schedule and preferences.

Combine with Rituals: Pair reminders with a specific ritual or cue that signals the beginning of your writing session.

Experiment with these reminder methods and choose the ones that best align with your habits and preferences. Combining multiple approaches may provide a well-rounded system to prompt and maintain your writing sessions for guitar composition in your musical diary.

BE FLEXIBLE

Be flexible with your schedule. Life may bring unexpected changes, and it's important to adapt. If you miss a scheduled session, don't be too hard on yourself—just resume the routine the next day.

Balancing flexibility with a routine in your musical diary for guitar composition is essential for maintaining a sustainable and adaptable creative practice. Life is unpredictable, and unforeseen circumstances may arise, making it important to be both flexible and consistent.

Here are some tips and examples on how to strike this balance and get back into the routine if you miss a session:

Establish a Core Routine

Tip: Define a core routine that includes your preferred writing times. This serves as a foundation while allowing flexibility.

Identify Non-Negotiables

Tip: Determine non-negotiable writing sessions that you commit to, even on busy days. These can be your anchor points in the routine.

Flexible Time Slots

Tip: Allow flexibility by having alternative time slots for writing sessions. If your morning routine is disrupted, you can switch to an afternoon or evening session.

Adjust Session Duration

Tip: If your schedule is tight, consider adjusting the duration of your writing sessions. A shorter but focused session is better than skipping altogether.

Consistent Starting Point

Tip: Maintain a consistent starting point or trigger for your writing sessions. Whether it's a specific time or a post-meal period, having a cue helps maintain routine elements.

Acknowledge without Guilt

Tip: If you miss a session, acknowledge it without guilt. Life is dynamic, and disruptions are natural. Be compassionate with yourself.

Reflect on the Why

Tip: Reflect on the reason for missing a session. Was it an unavoidable commitment, unexpected event, or lack of motivation? Understanding the cause helps prevent recurrence.

Reevaluate Goals

Tip: Periodically reassess your goals and adjust them based on changing circumstances. Flexibility includes adapting your routine to evolving needs.

Start Small After a Break

Tip: If you miss multiple sessions, ease back into your routine with shorter, manageable sessions. Starting small helps re-establish the habit.

Use a Trigger Activity

Tip: Incorporate a trigger activity before your writing sessions to signal the start of your routine. It could be a brief warm-up, a favorite song, or a specific ritual.

Set a Reentry Plan

Tip: Have a plan for reentering your routine after a break. Define specific actions or goals for the first few sessions to regain momentum.

Schedule a Return Session

Tip: Schedule your next writing session immediately after a break. This sets a clear intention to resume and minimizes the risk of prolonged disruptions.

Recommit Publicly

Tip: If you share your goals with a friend, family member, or online community, publicly recommitting after a break adds a layer of accountability.

Celebrate the Return

Tip: Celebrate your successful return to your routine. Recognize the effort it takes to reestablish consistency and acknowledge your commitment.

Reflect on Adjustments

Tip: Reflect on any adjustments needed in your routine to prevent future breaks. It could involve tweaking your schedule, setting realistic goals, or addressing potential obstacles.

Adapt as Necessary

Tip: Be adaptable and willing to make adjustments. If a particular time slot consistently leads to missed sessions, consider shifting your routine to a more feasible period.

Use a Tracker or Journal

Tip: Keep a tracker or journal to log your writing sessions. This visual representation of your consistency can motivate you to get back on track after a break.

Explore New Inspiration

Tip: Introduce new sources of inspiration after a break. This could be exploring different genres, learning a new technique, or collaborating with other musicians.

Reestablish Rituals

Tip: Reestablish any rituals or cues that were part of your routine before the break. These can help rekindle the mindset and motivation associated with your writing sessions.

Stay Positive

Tip: Maintain a positive mindset. Every journey has its ups and downs. Focus on the progress you make rather than dwelling on missed sessions.

By finding a balance between flexibility and routine and implementing strategies to get back into the routine after a break, you can foster a sustainable and resilient approach to writing in your musical diary for guitar composition. Life is full of changes, and adapting your routine with a positive and proactive mindset will contribute to long-term success.

Establish Accountability

Share your writing schedule with a friend, family member, or fellow musician who can provide encouragement and accountability. Knowing that someone else is aware of your commitment can help you stay on track.

Establishing accountability can significantly contribute to your consistency in making entries in your musical diary for guitar composition. Having a sense of responsibility to yourself and potentially others can help maintain motivation and commitment to your creative practice.

Here are some tips and examples on how to establish accountability:

Share Your Goals with Someone

Tip: Share your musical diary goals with a friend, family member, or fellow musician who can provide support and encouragement.

Example: Tell a friend about your commitment to making daily guitar composition entries and ask them to check in with you regularly to discuss your progress.

Join a Creative Community

Tip: Participate in online or local creative communities related to music and composition where members share their progress and goals.

Example: Join a forum, social media group, or community platform where musicians and composers discuss their musical journeys. Share your goals and updates regularly.

Collaborate with Others

Tip: Collaborate on musical projects or compositions with other musicians. The collaborative aspect adds a layer of accountability.

Example: Initiate a collaboration with a fellow guitarist or musician, setting deadlines for each other to contribute to the joint project.

Set Public Commitments

Tip: Make your goals public by sharing them on social media or personal blogs. Public commitments can create a sense of external accountability.

Example: Post on your social media accounts about your commitment to making regular entries in your musical diary, and provide updates on your progress.

Create a Progress Journal

Tip: Maintain a public or private journal documenting your musical journey, including your goals, challenges, and achievements.

Example: Use a blog or a private document to journal your experiences with guitar composition, and regularly update it with your progress.

Use Accountability Apps

Tip: Use apps designed to help you stay accountable, whether through goal tracking, habit-building, or reminders.

Example: Apps like HabitBull, Strides, or Streaks allow you to set and track goals, providing visual cues for your progress.

Set Regular Check-Ins

Tip: Establish regular check-in points with an accountability partner or group to discuss your achievements, challenges, and plans.

Example: Schedule weekly or monthly video calls with a friend or fellow musician to review your musical diary entries and discuss your compositions.

Participate in Challenges

Tip: Engage in musical challenges or competitions that require regular submissions. These can provide a structured framework for accountability.

Example: Join online music challenges or competitions where participants submit compositions regularly. The deadlines and community engagement foster accountability.

Reward-Based System

Tip: Implement a reward-based system for achieving your musical diary goals. Treat yourself when you reach milestones.

Example: Set specific milestones, and reward yourself with something meaningful, such as a new piece of gear, a favorite treat, or a break to enjoy a favorite activity.

Track and Share Progress

Tip: Regularly track and share your progress. This can be done through social media updates, blog posts, or even a dedicated section in your musical diary.

Example: Create a visual timeline or infographic showcasing your musical journey, milestones, and notable compositions. Share this with your network.

Accountability Contracts

Tip: Create a written accountability contract outlining your goals, commitments, and consequences for not meeting them. Share it with someone who will hold you accountable.

Example: Draft a simple contract stating your intentions, sign it, and give a copy to a trusted friend. Agree on consequences for not adhering to your commitments.

Use a Tracking System

Tip: Implement a tracking system that allows you to visually see your consistency over time. This could be a calendar, a habit tracker, or a dedicated app.

Example: Use a wall calendar to mark each day you make a musical diary entry. Seeing a chain of marks can be a powerful motivator.

Engage in Regular Reflection

Tip: Reflect regularly on your progress and challenges. This introspective process helps reinforce your commitment.

Example: Dedicate time each week to reflect on your musical diary entries, identifying patterns, areas for improvement, and celebrating achievements.

Invest in a Music Teacher or Mentor

Tip: If feasible, work with a music teacher or mentor who can provide guidance, feedback, and support.

Example: Enroll in guitar lessons or seek mentorship from an experienced musician who can guide your musical journey and hold you accountable.

Create a Personal Challenge

Tip: Design personal challenges or projects that align with your musical goals. Share these challenges with others to increase accountability.

Example: Start a 30-day composition challenge where you commit to creating a short piece every day. Share your progress with your social circle.

Tips for Effective Accountability

Be Clear About Goals: Clearly define your musical diary goals to ensure your accountability partners understand your intentions.

Regularly Communicate: Stay in regular communication with your accountability partners, providing updates and seeking feedback.

Celebrate Achievements: Acknowledge and celebrate milestones and achievements, reinforcing positive behavior.

Adjust as Needed: Periodically reassess your accountability methods and make adjustments based on your evolving needs.

By implementing these accountability strategies and finding a system that works best for you, you can enhance your commitment to making regular entries in your musical diary for guitar composition. Having a support system and external accountability can turn your creative aspirations into tangible achievements.

REFLECT AND ADJUST

Regularly reflect on your writing schedule. Assess whether the frequency and timing align with your creative needs. Be open to adjusting your schedule if necessary.

Regular reflection on your writing schedule in your musical diary for guitar composition is crucial for ensuring that the frequency and timing align with your creative needs.

Here are some questions to ask yourself during these reflective sessions, along with tips and examples to help you assess and adjust your writing schedule:

Am I Meeting My Goals?

Question: Are you consistently achieving the goals you set for your musical diary entries and guitar compositions?

Tip: Review your initial goals and assess whether your current writing schedule contributes to meeting these objectives. If adjustments are needed, consider modifying your routine.

Does the Frequency Suit My Lifestyle?

Question: Is the frequency of your writing sessions realistic given your current lifestyle and commitments?

Tip: Consider your daily or weekly responsibilities, work schedule, and other obligations. Ensure that your writing frequency aligns with what you can realistically sustain over the long term.

Is the Timing Optimal for Creativity?

Question: Are you scheduling writing sessions during times when you are most creatively inspired and focused?

Tip: Identify your peak creative hours. If possible, schedule your writing sessions during these times to leverage your natural creative energy.

Do I Feel Rushed or Overwhelmed?

Question: Do you feel rushed or overwhelmed during your writing sessions, or do you have sufficient time to explore ideas?

Tip: Assess whether your current schedule allows for a comfortable and immersive creative process. If you feel rushed, consider extending the duration of your sessions or adjusting the timing.

Is There a Consistent Starting Ritual?

Question: Do you have a consistent starting ritual or cue that helps you transition into your writing sessions?

Tip: Establishing a ritual, such as playing a specific chord progression or listening to a favorite piece, can signal the beginning of your creative process and enhance focus.

Am I Balancing Structure and Flexibility?

Question: Are you finding a balance between having a structured routine and being flexible to accommodate unexpected changes?

Tip: Ensure that your schedule is adaptable to life's unpredictabilities while maintaining a level of structure that supports regular creative expression.

Am I Experimenting with Different Times?

Question: Have you experimented with writing sessions at different times of the day to assess when you are most productive and inspired?

Tip: Try writing during various time slots and observe when you feel most connected to your creative flow. Adjust your schedule accordingly based on your findings.

Are External Distractions Minimized?

Question: Are you able to minimize external distractions during your writing sessions?

Tip: Evaluate your environment for potential distractions and consider implementing strategies to create a focused space. This may involve choosing a quiet location, using noise-canceling headphones, or setting boundaries with others.

Do I Need to Adjust Session Duration?

Question: Is the duration of your writing sessions conducive to your creative process, or do you need to make adjustments?

Tip: Assess whether the current session length allows for meaningful exploration and development. If necessary, experiment with shorter or longer durations to find the optimal balance.

Is Progress Consistent Over Time?

Question: Are you consistently making progress in your guitar compositions, or do you notice stagnation or regression?

Tip: Use your musical diary entries to track your progress over time. If you observe patterns of stagnation, consider adjusting your writing schedule to inject new inspiration or challenges.

Are There Patterns of Resistance?

Question: Do you notice patterns of resistance or procrastination during certain times of the day or week?

Tip: Identify potential resistance points and explore the underlying reasons. Adjust your schedule to minimize resistance, whether it's by changing the time or incorporating motivational strategies.

Am I Enjoying the Process?

Question: Are you enjoying the creative process, or does it feel like a chore?

Tip: Regularly assess your overall satisfaction with your musical diary entries. If the process becomes monotonous, consider introducing variety, exploring new genres, or collaborating with others to reignite passion.

Do I Need to Reevaluate Goals?

Question: Have your musical and creative goals evolved, necessitating a reassessment of your current writing schedule?

Tip: Periodically revisit your long-term goals and adjust your writing schedule to align with your evolving aspirations. This ensures that your routine remains relevant and purposeful.

Are External Commitments Impacting My Schedule?

Question: Are external commitments, such as work or personal obligations, impacting your writing schedule?

Tip: Be mindful of external factors that may affect your availability for writing sessions. Adjust your schedule accordingly to accommodate changes in commitments.

Am I Open to Experimentation?

Question: Are you open to experimenting with different schedules, environments, or creative approaches to enhance your writing sessions?

Tip: Embrace a spirit of experimentation and be willing to adapt your schedule based on the insights gained through exploration.

Tips for Effective Reflection

Set Regular Reflection Sessions: Schedule dedicated time for regular reflection on your writing schedule, perhaps at the end of each week or month.

Document Insights: Keep notes in your musical diary about your reflections, insights, and any adjustments you make to your schedule.

Be Open to Change: Be open to making changes to your writing schedule based on your reflections. Flexibility is key to finding a routine that truly suits your creative needs.

Celebrate Progress: Acknowledge and celebrate your achievements and progress during your reflection sessions. Positive reinforcement contributes to motivation and commitment.

By regularly asking yourself these questions and engaging in thoughtful reflection, you can fine-tune your writing schedule in your musical diary for guitar composition to better align with your creative needs and aspirations. Adjustments made based on this self-assessment can lead to a more fulfilling and productive creative practice.

CELEBRATE MILESTONES

Acknowledge and celebrate milestones in your writing journey. This could be reaching a certain number of entries, completing a section of your composition, or any other significant achievement.

Acknowledging and celebrating milestones in your writing journey for guitar composition is a meaningful way to recognize your progress and stay motivated. Setting specific milestones helps you track your achievements and provides a sense of accomplishment. Here are some milestones to consider for your musical diary and ideas on how to celebrate them:

Completion of a Composition

Milestone: Finish composing an entire piece, whether it's a song, instrumental, or part of a larger project.

Celebration Ideas: Record a performance or demo of the composition. Share the completed piece with friends, family, or online communities. Reflect on the journey and note key learnings in your musical diary.

Consistent Daily/Weekly Entries

Milestone: Achieve a streak of consistent daily or weekly entries in your musical diary.

Celebration Ideas: Treat yourself to a special practice session or play your favorite guitar piece.

Share your accomplishment on social media to receive encouragement. Reward yourself with a small indulgence, such as enjoying a favorite snack or beverage.

Learning a New Technique

Milestone: Master a new guitar technique or incorporate a challenging element into your compositions.

Celebration Ideas: Record a video demonstrating the technique. Share your achievement with a music teacher or fellow musicians for feedback. Treat yourself to a concert ticket or music-related item you've been eyeing.

Positive Feedback or Recognition

Milestone: Receive positive feedback, compliments, or recognition for your compositions.

Celebration Ideas: Compile positive comments and create a dedicated section in your musical diary. Express gratitude to those who provided feedback. Consider collaborating with others or seeking opportunities for your work to be featured.

Experimentation with a New Genre or Style

Milestone: Explore and successfully incorporate a new genre or musical style into your compositions.

Celebration Ideas: Record a medley or compilation showcasing your exploration of different styles. Share your experimentation on social media and engage with others who appreciate diversity in music. Attend a live performance or listen to artists within the genre you explored.

Setting and Achieving Quarterly Goals

Milestone: Establish and accomplish specific quarterly goals related to your musical diary entries.

Celebration Ideas: Reflect on the achievements and challenges of the quarter in your musical diary. Share your progress with a mentor or accountability partner. Plan a reward or treat yourself to a musical-related purchase.

Completion of a Learning Challenge

Milestone: Successfully complete a learning challenge, such as a 30-day composition challenge or technical exercise.

Celebration Ideas: Compile a compilation of your challenge entries. Share your journey on social media or music forums. Treat yourself to a musical workshop or online course as a reward.

Performing in Public

Milestone: Have the courage to perform your composition or play your guitar in front of an audience, whether it's online or at a local venue.

Celebration Ideas: Record the performance and share it on **platform**s like YouTube or Instagram. Reflect on the experience in your musical diary, noting personal growth. Celebrate with friends or family after the performance.

Successful Collaboration

Milestone: Collaborate with another musician or artist on a project or composition.

Celebration Ideas: Showcase the collaborative work on social media or a dedicated platform. Send a personalized thank-you note or gift to your collaborator. Plan a small celebration or jam session together.

Exploration of a New Creative Process

Milestone: Experiment with a new creative process or approach to your guitar composition.

Celebration Ideas: Document your exploration in your musical diary. Share insights with fellow musicians or in online forums. Incorporate elements from the new creative process into future compositions.

Reaching a Follower Milestone

Milestone: Achieve a specific milestone in terms of followers or subscribers on your music platforms.

Celebration Ideas: Create a special post or video thanking your followers for their support. Consider hosting a live session or Q&A to engage with your audience. Collaborate with other musicians to cross-promote and celebrate together.

Adaptation to Feedback and Improvement

Milestone: Show an ability to adapt to feedback and consistently improve your compositions.

Celebration Ideas: Highlight specific improvements in your musical diary. Seek feedback from a mentor or music teacher and incorporate their suggestions. Acknowledge and celebrate the iterative nature of the creative process.

Tips for Effective Celebration

Personalize the Celebration: Tailor your celebrations to align with your interests and preferences.

Document the Milestone: Capture the milestone in your musical diary, including your emotions, reflections, and any notable achievements.

Share the Joy: If comfortable, share your celebrations with your musical community or social circle to receive encouragement and support.

Set Future Goals: Use celebrations as opportunities to set new goals and continue progressing in your musical journey.

By establishing and celebrating these milestones, you not only recognize your achievements but also cultivate a positive and motivating environment for your musical diary entries and guitar compositions. Celebrations contribute to a sense of fulfillment, encourage ongoing dedication, and make your creative journey more enjoyable.

USE A TRACKING SYSTEM

Implement a tracking system to monitor your progress. Whether it's a calendar, habit-tracking app, or a simple checklist, having a visual representation of your consistency can be motivating.

Tracking your progress in your musical diary for guitar composition is crucial for maintaining motivation and staying focused on your goals. There are various software, apps, and methods that can help you effectively track your musical journey.

Digital Note-Taking Apps

Examples: Evernote, Microsoft OneNote, Google Keep

Use digital note-taking apps to create dedicated entries for each composition or milestone. Organize your notes by date, project, or theme, making it easy to track your progress over time.

Spreadsheets

Examples: Microsoft Excel, Google Sheets

Create a spreadsheet to log details such as composition titles, dates, key elements, and milestones achieved. You can use columns for different aspects like tempo, mood, and techniques explored.

Task Management Apps

Examples: Todoist, Microsoft To Do, Trello

Set up tasks or cards for each step of your composition process. This helps you break down larger goals into manageable tasks, providing a clear overview of your progress.

Journaling Apps

Examples: Day One, Journey, Penzu
Use dedicated journaling apps to create detailed entries about your daily or weekly progress. These apps often allow you to attach media, making them ideal for documenting your musical journey.

Music-Specific Apps

Examples: Soundtrap, GarageBand, BandLab
Utilize music creation apps to track the evolution of your compositions. Save different versions, record snippets, and document your thoughts directly within these platforms.

Habit-Tracking Apps

Examples: HabitBull, Streaks, Habitica
Monitor your consistency in making musical diary entries or working on compositions with habit-tracking apps. Create a habit for your daily or weekly writing sessions and track your streaks.

Calendar Apps

Examples: Google Calendar, Apple Calendar, Microsoft Outlook

Schedule your composition sessions as events in your calendar. Include details such as goals, themes, or techniques you plan to explore during each session.

Goal-Setting Apps

Examples: Strides, Goalify, Lifetick

Set specific musical goals and milestones using goal-setting apps. Track your progress toward these goals and celebrate achievements along the way.

Voice Recorder Apps

Examples: Voice Memos (iOS), Easy Voice Recorder (Android), Audacity

Use voice recorder apps to capture your thoughts, ideas, or reflections on your compositions. This can serve as an auditory diary and a way to document your creative process.

Social Media Platforms

Examples: Instagram, X (Twitter), Facebook, Tik Tok

Description: Share snippets or updates of your musical journey on social media. Use dedicated hashtags to catalog your progress and receive feedback from a wider community.

Mind Mapping Tools

Examples: MindMeister, XMind, SimpleMind

Create visual mind maps to outline your composition ideas, themes, and connections. These tools help you visualize the structure of your musical projects.

GitHub or Version Control Systems

Examples: GitHub, Bitbucket

If you're comfortable with version control systems, use platforms like GitHub to track changes in your compositions. This is particularly useful for collaborative projects.

Customized Tracking Apps

Examples: Notion, Airtable

Build your custom tracking system using versatile apps like Notion or Airtable. Tailor the database or workspace to fit your specific needs for tracking progress.

Camera/Video Recording

Examples: Smartphone camera, dedicated video camera

Record video snippets of your practice sessions, performances, or reflections. Keep these recordings organized in folders or cloud storage for easy access.

Custom Spreadsheet Templates

Examples: Tiller Money, Vertex42

Explore pre-designed spreadsheet templates for goal tracking, habit-building, or project management.

Adapt these templates to suit your musical diary tracking needs.

Tips for Effective Progress Tracking

Consistency: Regularly update your chosen tracking system to ensure accurate documentation.

Reflect: Use your tracking system as a tool for reflection, noting challenges, breakthroughs, and lessons learned.

Stay Flexible: Adapt your tracking method as needed. Experiment with different systems until you find one that aligns with your workflow.

Celebrate Milestones: Acknowledge and celebrate achievements recorded in your tracking system to stay motivated.

Experiment with these tools and methods to find the tracking system that best suits your preferences and helps you stay organized and motivated in your musical diary for guitar composition.

ENJOY THE PROCESS

Embrace the writing process as a form of self-expression and exploration. Enjoy the opportunity to delve into your thoughts, emotions, and musical ideas.

Embracing the writing process in your musical diary for guitar composition as a form of self-expression and exploration is essential for fostering a positive and fulfilling creative experience. Instead of viewing it as an unpleasant chore, consider it an opportunity to connect with your musical identity, experiment with ideas, and document your artistic journey.

Here are tips and examples to help you embrace the writing process:

Shift Your Mindset

Tip: Approach your musical diary with a positive and open mindset. Recognize it as a personal space for self-expression, learning, and growth rather than a task to be completed.

Example: Before starting a writing session, take a moment to reflect on the joy of creating music and the unique opportunity your diary provides for capturing your creative thoughts.

Set Intentional Goals

Tip: Establish clear and intentional goals for each writing session. Focus on aspects of self-expression, such as experimenting with a new chord progression or capturing a specific emotion.

Example: Instead of setting a goal like "write a complete song," set an intention like "explore different fingerstyle patterns" or "express feelings of nostalgia in a short melody."

Freeform Exploration

Tip: Allow yourself to engage in freeform exploration during your writing sessions. Give space for spontaneous creativity and don't worry about adhering to strict structures.

Example: Dedicate a portion of your session to improvisation, letting your fingers guide you on the fretboard without the pressure of a predetermined outcome.

Capture Emotions and Stories

Tip: Use your musical diary to capture not only technical details but also the emotions and stories behind your compositions. Describe the feelings or events that inspired your musical ideas.

Example: Write about a recent experience, a vivid dream, or a powerful emotion that you want to convey through your guitar composition. Connect the personal narrative to your musical expressions.

Reflect on Your Progress

Tip: Regularly reflect on your musical journey within your diary. Celebrate milestones, acknowledge challenges, and recognize the progress you've made, fostering a sense of achievement.

Example: Take time to revisit earlier entries and notice how your style, skills, and creative voice have evolved over time. Reflecting on your growth can be a powerful motivator.

Create a Visual Element

Tip: Enhance the visual aspect of your musical diary. Sketch or doodle alongside your written entries to add a visual representation of your emotions or musical ideas.

Example: If you're struggling to express a concept in words, create a simple visual representation using symbols, shapes, or diagrams to convey your ideas visually.

Experiment with Different Genres

Tip: Break away from routine by exploring different genres and styles in your musical diary. Embrace the diversity of musical expression to keep the process fresh and exciting.

Example: If you primarily compose in a specific genre, challenge yourself to experiment with elements from a completely different musical style. This exploration can lead to unique and unexpected compositions.

Celebrate Imperfections

Tip: Embrace imperfections as part of the creative process. Recognize that not every session needs to result in a polished masterpiece, and allow room for experimentation and mistakes.

Example: If you make a mistake or encounter a challenge during your writing session, see it as an opportunity to learn and grow. Use imperfections as stepping stones toward improvement.

Incorporate Multimedia Elements

Tip: Expand your expressive range by incorporating multimedia elements into your musical diary. Embed audio recordings, videos, or images that complement your written descriptions.

Example: If you're working on a specific technique, record a short video clip demonstrating your progress. This adds a dynamic and immersive dimension to your diary entries.

Share and Seek Feedback

Tip: Share selected entries from your musical diary with friends, mentors, or online communities. Seeking feedback and sharing your creative process can foster a sense of connection and encouragement.

Example: Post snippets of your compositions on social media or music forums, inviting others to share their thoughts. Embrace constructive feedback as an opportunity for growth.

Dedicate Time to Exploration

Tip: Designate specific writing sessions solely for exploration and experimentation. Free yourself from the pressure of creating a finished piece and focus on discovering new sounds and techniques.

Example: Allocate one session per week to explore a new guitar tuning, experiment with alternate playing techniques, or delve into unconventional chord progressions without the expectation of a final product.

Establish Rituals

Tip: Create rituals or routines that signal the beginning of your writing sessions. This can help shift your mindset into a creative mode and make the process more enjoyable.

Example: Before each session, listen to a favorite piece of music, light a candle, or take a moment to breathe deeply. These rituals can create a positive and focused environment for self-expression.

Collaborate with Others

Tip: Collaborate with fellow musicians or artists to infuse new perspectives into your creative process. Joint projects can provide fresh inspiration and make the writing process more dynamic.

Example: Partner with a lyricist, vocalist, or another instrumentalist to collaborate on a composition. The exchange of ideas and collaborative energy can enhance your creative exploration.

Attend Workshops and Events

Tip: Participate in music workshops, events, or seminars to expose yourself to diverse influences and broaden your musical palette. These experiences can fuel your creative expression.

Example: Attend a guitar masterclass, music festival, or online webinar to gain insights from other musicians and discover new approaches to composition.

Express Your Unique Voice

Tip: Recognize and celebrate your unique musical voice. Embrace the qualities that make your compositions distinct, and don't be afraid to infuse your personality into your writing.

Example: Identify elements in your compositions that resonate with your personal style. Whether it's a signature chord progression, melodic motif, or thematic preference, let these aspects shine through.

Tips for Consistent Embrace of the Writing Process

Be Patient: Allow yourself the time and space to grow as a musician. The writing process is a journey, and each step contributes to your artistic development.

Celebrate Small Wins: Acknowledge and celebrate small achievements and breakthroughs during your writing sessions. These victories contribute to the overall joy of the creative process.

Adapt and Evolve: Be open to evolving your writing process. Experiment with new techniques, styles, or approaches, and adapt your methods based on what brings you the most satisfaction.

Connect with Others: Engage with fellow musicians, attend open mic nights, or join online communities to share experiences and draw inspiration from the diverse musical journeys of others.

Record Musical Ideas and Inspirations

Whenever a musical idea or inspiration strikes, jot it down in your diary. This could be a melody, a chord progression, a rhythm pattern, or any other musical element that resonates with you. Capture the essence of moments through musical notations, chords, and descriptive words.

By embracing the writing process in your musical diary as a form of self-expression and exploration, you can transform it into a deeply enriching and enjoyable experience. Cultivate a positive mindset, experiment with different elements, and celebrate the unique journey that is your musical diary for guitar composition.

Remember that establishing a writing routine is a gradual process, and it's okay to make adjustments along the way. The key is to make writing in your musical diary a pleasurable and meaningful part of your creative journey.

Date Each Entry

Begin each entry by dating it. This allows you to trace the progression of your thoughts and experiences over time, providing context to your creative journey.

Dating each entry in your musical diary for guitar composition serves several important purposes, enhancing the effectiveness and value of your diary over time.

Here are some reasons why dating each entry is beneficial, along with examples to illustrate their significance:

Chronological Progress Tracking

Importance: Dating entries allows you to track the chronological progression of your musical journey. It provides a clear timeline of your creative process, helping you see how your skills, ideas, and techniques evolve over time.

Example: If you start a new composition on January 15th and revisit it a month later, you can observe the development from initial concepts to more refined ideas by comparing the dated entries.

Reflection on Growth and Milestones

Importance: Dating entries facilitates reflection on your growth and milestones. It allows you to revisit specific points in your musical diary and celebrate achievements, whether they are small victories or significant breakthroughs.

Example: On March 10th, you might note that you successfully incorporated a challenging chord progression into a composition. Reflecting on this entry later helps you appreciate your progress.

Identification of Patterns and Trends

Importance: By dating entries, you can identify patterns and trends in your creative process. This helps you understand your most productive periods, common challenges, and the factors influencing your musical exploration.

Example: If you consistently experiment with new techniques during a particular month each year, you may notice a pattern that aligns with your creative cycles.

Context for Emotional Expression

Importance: Dating entries provides context for emotional expression. It allows you to connect your creative output with specific events, feelings, or experiences, enhancing the emotional depth of your musical diary.

Example: If you compose a piece on February 14th, you might associate it with the emotions you experienced on Valentine's Day, creating a richer narrative within your diary.

Documentation of Challenges and Solutions

Importance: Dating entries helps document challenges faced during your musical composition journey and the solutions you implement. This documentation aids in learning from past experiences and refining your approach.

Example: If you encounter difficulty in creating a seamless transition between sections on April 5th, you can revisit the entry to review the strategies you employed to address the challenge.

Enhanced Organization and Navigation

Importance: Dating entries contributes to enhanced organization and navigation within your musical diary. It makes it easier to locate specific compositions, ideas, or reflections, streamlining the overall accessibility of your creative documentation.

Example: When you want to find a particular piece composed in June, you can quickly navigate to entries from that month, simplifying the retrieval process.

Facilitation of Goal Setting and Planning

Importance: Dating entries facilitates goal setting and planning by offering a temporal reference point. It allows you to set realistic timelines for achieving specific milestones and helps you stay accountable to your musical aspirations.

Example: If you set a goal to complete a composition by May 20th, dating entries in your musical diary helps you monitor progress toward that target date.

Contextual Understanding for Collaborations

Importance: If you collaborate with others or share your musical diary, dating entries provides contextual understanding for collaborators. It helps them grasp the timeline and context of your compositions, making collaboration more seamless.

Example: When sharing entries with a collaborator, they can see when specific ideas were introduced, making it easier for them to align their contributions with the overall timeline.

Measurement of Consistency and Habit Building

Importance: Dating entries allows you to measure your consistency and progress in forming creative habits. It serves as a visual record of your dedication and commitment to regular musical exploration.

Example: If you make a note that you've written in your musical diary every Monday for the past three months, you can visually see your commitment to the habit.

Historical Reference for Inspiration

Importance: Dating entries creates a historical reference for inspiration. When looking back through your musical diary, you can draw inspiration from past ideas, compositions, and reflections to fuel new creative endeavors.

Example: While exploring entries from a year ago, you may rediscover a melodic motif that sparks a fresh idea for a current composition.

Effective Time Management

Importance: Dating entries helps you manage your time effectively. It provides a tangible record of how you allocate time to your musical pursuits, aiding in the optimization of your creative schedule.

Example: If you notice that you tend to be more productive during evening sessions, you can adjust your schedule to prioritize creative work during those hours.

Facilitation of Feedback and Critique

Importance: When seeking feedback or critiques from others, dating entries provides context for reviewers. It helps them understand when specific elements or challenges arose, enabling more targeted and constructive feedback.

Example: If you share a composition with a mentor, they can reference the date to understand the creative context and offer insights accordingly.

Documentation of External Influences

Importance: Dating entries allows you to document external influences that may impact your compositions. Whether it's a book, a concert, or a personal experience, dating entries helps connect your creative output with external inspirations.

Example: If you attend a guitar workshop on May 1st, you can note the influence it had on your subsequent compositions throughout the month.

Record of Instrumental Changes

Importance: If you make changes to your instrument or experiment with different guitars or equipment, dating entries helps you keep a record. This is particularly useful in understanding how different instruments affect your compositions.

Example: If you switch to a new guitar on July 10th, you can observe how the change in instrument influences the tone and style of your compositions.

Memory Aid for Performances

Importance: When preparing for performances, dating entries can serve as a memory aid. It helps you recall the timeline of composition creation, allowing you to revisit specific pieces and prepare accordingly.

Example: Before a live performance on September 5th, you can review the entries related to the compositions you plan to play, refreshing your memory on the creative context.

Tips for Effective Dating of Entries

Consistency: Date each entry consistently, preferably at the beginning of the session or reflection.

Include Time: Consider including the time of day for entries to provide additional context.

Use a Standard Format: Adopt a standardized date format (e.g., MM/DD/YYYY) for uniformity.

By consistently dating each entry in your musical diary for guitar composition, you create a comprehensive and organized record of your creative journey. This chronological documentation not only helps you reflect on your progress but also serves as a valuable resource for future inspiration, collaboration, and personal growth.

SOURCES OF INSPIRATION AND IDEAS

Identifying sources of inspiration and ideas for your musical diary entries are important to advance the generation of your guitar composition. Opening your mind's door by asking yourself the right questions can unlock a deluge of creativity.

WHAT INSPIRED THIS MUSICAL IDEA?

Identify the source of inspiration for the musical idea. Was it a specific emotion, experience, or external stimulus that triggered this idea?

Identifying the source of inspiration for the musical ideas you write down in your musical diary for guitar composition can enhance your understanding of your creative process and provide valuable insights into your artistic influences.

Here are some tips and tricks to help you identify the sources of inspiration:

Reflect on Emotional States

Tip: Consider your emotional state when a musical idea strikes. Your feelings, moods, and experiences can be powerful sources of inspiration.

Example: If you notice a melancholic melody emerging, reflect on recent experiences that might have evoked feelings of sadness, nostalgia, or introspection.

Explore Personal Experiences

Tip: Look into your personal experiences for inspiration. Events, relationships, or significant moments in your life can serve as rich sources of creative material.

Example: If you find yourself creating a lively and upbeat composition, it may be influenced by a recent positive experience or celebration in your life.

Analyze External Influences

Tip: Be mindful of external influences such as books, movies, art, or nature. Analyze your surroundings to identify elements that might be subtly influencing your musical ideas.

Example: If you've recently read a novel with a compelling storyline, your composition might draw inspiration from the emotions and themes portrayed in the book.

Track Listening Habits

Tip: Pay attention to your listening habits. The music you've been exposed to, whether intentionally or subconsciously, can play a role in shaping your musical ideas.

Example: If you've been listening to a lot of jazz, you may notice elements of improvisation or specific chord progressions influencing your compositions.

Note Technical Influences

Tip: Consider technical aspects that inspire you. It could be a specific guitar technique, a chord progression, or a unique way of approaching rhythm.

Example: If you incorporate fingerstyle techniques after attending a workshop or watching a tutorial, you can trace the technical influence back to that learning experience.

Explore Cultural Influences

Tip: Explore how your cultural background or exposure to different cultures may influence your musical ideas. Cultural elements can contribute unique flavors to your compositions.

Example: If you integrate flamenco-style guitar playing, it might be inspired by your cultural heritage or exposure to flamenco music.

Document Inspirational Sparks

Tip: Keep a record of moments when inspiration strikes. Jot down not only the musical idea but also the circumstances, emotions, or external stimuli that triggered the inspiration.

Example: If you suddenly come up with a beautiful melody while taking a walk in the park, note the surroundings, weather, and any specific sights or sounds that contributed to the inspiration.

Analyze Subconscious Influences

Tip: Pay attention to your subconscious influences. Sometimes, inspiration comes from elements you might not be consciously aware of at first.

Example: If you notice a recurring motif in your compositions, it could be a subconscious reflection of your personal preferences or influences from your musical background.

Experiment with Cross-Artistic Influences

Tip: Experiment with cross-artistic influences by drawing inspiration from other art forms. Visual arts, poetry, or dance can stimulate creative ideas for your guitar compositions.

Example: After visiting an art gallery, you might find inspiration in the colors, shapes, or emotions conveyed in a painting that translates into your guitar compositions.

Seek Moments of Solitude

Tip: Create moments of solitude to foster self-reflection. Quiet, contemplative moments can reveal subtle inspirations that may not be apparent in the noise of everyday life.

Example: Taking a quiet walk or spending time alone in nature might trigger introspective musical ideas influenced by the peaceful surroundings.

Experiment with Different Tunings

Tip: Experiment with different guitar tunings as a way to explore new sonic possibilities. A change in tuning can lead to fresh ideas and inspiration.

Example: If you switch to an open tuning, the unique harmonic resonances may spark new ideas that draw inspiration from the altered sound palette.

Keep a Visual Inspiration Board

Tip: Create a visual inspiration board where you collect images, quotes, or symbols that resonate with you. This board can serve as a visual representation of your sources of inspiration.

Example: If you're drawn to images of vast landscapes, incorporate the sense of expansiveness and openness into your compositions.

Stay Open to Serendipity

Tip: Stay open to serendipitous moments. Inspiration can strike unexpectedly, and being receptive to the unexpected can lead to unique and spontaneous creative ideas.

Example: If a musical idea comes to you while idly strumming your guitar, embrace the spontaneity and allow it to shape your composition.

Join Collaborative Projects

Tip: Collaborate with other musicians or artists. Engaging in collaborative projects exposes you to different perspectives and can be a rich source of inspiration.

Example: Collaborating with a lyricist might inspire new musical ideas based on the themes or emotions conveyed in the lyrics.

Periodically Review and Reflect

Tip: Periodically review and reflect on your musical diary entries. This practice allows you to connect the dots between your musical ideas and the sources of inspiration that influenced them.

Example: During a reflection session, you might discover patterns where certain environments, emotions, or external stimuli consistently contribute to your creative process.

Tips for Being Better Attuned to Sources of Inspiration

Cultivate Awareness: Cultivate mindfulness and awareness of your surroundings, emotions, and experiences during your creative sessions.

Diversify Your Inputs: Expose yourself to a diverse range of influences, whether it's through different genres of music, cultural experiences, or other art forms.

Document External Influences: Make a habit of noting external influences as you encounter them, whether it's a movie, a book, or a conversation.

Regularly Revisit Influences: Periodically revisit and explore the influences that have left a lasting impact on your musical journey.

By adopting these tips and tricks, you can develop a heightened awareness of the sources of inspiration for your musical ideas. Regular reflection, exploration of diverse influences, and staying attuned to your emotions and surroundings will contribute to a deeper understanding of your creative process.

WHAT EMOTIONS DOES THIS IDEA CONVEY?

Explore the emotional landscape of the musical idea. What feelings or moods does it evoke? How can you describe the emotional impact in words?

Exploring the emotional landscape of your musical ideas and effectively conveying emotions through words in your musical diary for guitar composition is a powerful way to deepen the impact of your compositions.

Here are some tips on how to explore and express emotions in your musical diary, along with examples of emotions and ways to pair them with musical ideas:

Identify Emotions

Tip: Begin by identifying the specific emotions you want to convey in your composition. Emotions can range from joy and excitement to melancholy and introspection.

Example Emotions:
Joy
Sadness
Love
Anger
Serenity
Nostalgia

Hope
Despair

Pair Emotions with Musical Elements

Tip: Consider how various musical elements can evoke specific emotions. Elements like tempo, dynamics, harmony, and rhythm can be tailored to convey different emotional nuances.

Example: To convey a sense of joy, you might use a lively tempo, bright major chords, and energetic strumming patterns. For sadness, slower tempos, minor chords, and softer dynamics can be more appropriate.

Use Descriptive Language

Tip: Use descriptive language in your musical diary to articulate the emotions you intend to express. Incorporate adjectives, metaphors, and vivid imagery to convey the emotional landscape.

Example: Instead of simply stating that a composition evokes sadness, describe it as *"a melancholic melody that weaves through the heart, echoing the somber beauty of a fading sunset."*

Explore Contrast in Dynamics

Tip: Experiment with dynamic contrast to heighten emotional impact. Varying between soft and loud passages can create tension and release, adding depth to the emotional narrative.

Example: In a composition conveying a range of emotions, utilize soft, delicate picking for introspective moments and build to powerful strumming or picking for moments of intensity.

Incorporate Expressive Techniques

Tip: Explore expressive guitar techniques to convey emotions. Techniques like vibrato, slides, bends, and hammer-ons can add nuance and emotion to your playing.

Example: Use gentle vibrato on sustained notes to add a touch of warmth and vulnerability to convey a sense of longing or passion.

Experiment with Tempo and Rhythm

Tip: Adjust the tempo and rhythm to match the emotional tone you want to convey. Faster tempos can convey excitement, while slower tempos may evoke introspection or sadness.

Example: A brisk, upbeat rhythm can evoke a sense of exhilaration, while a slower, steady rhythm can create a contemplative or meditative mood.

Utilize Harmony and Chord Progressions

Tip: Experiment with different harmonies and chord progressions to evoke specific emotions. Major chords often convey happiness, while minor chords can evoke a sense of melancholy.

Example: A progression from C major to G major can create a bright, uplifting feel, while a progression from

A minor to E minor may evoke a more contemplative and introspective mood.

Consider Song Structure

Tip: The structure of your composition can contribute to the emotional journey. Experiment with the arrangement of verses, choruses, and instrumental breaks to build tension and release.

Example: Build anticipation by introducing a recurring melody in the verses and reach an emotional climax in the chorus before providing resolution in the final section.

Reflect on Personal Experiences

Tip: Draw on personal experiences to infuse authenticity into your emotional expressions. Reflect on moments of joy, sorrow, love, or conflict and channel those emotions into your compositions.

Example: If you're composing a piece inspired by a happy memory, recall the specific details of that moment and translate them into musical motifs.

Capture Transitions between Emotions

Tip: Explore the transitions between different emotions within a composition. Capture the ebb and flow of emotional intensity to create a dynamic and engaging musical journey.

Example: Transition from a serene, contemplative section to a burst of passionate intensity, creating a contrast that adds emotional depth.

Use Imagery in Your Writing

Tip: Incorporate vivid imagery in your written reflections to enhance emotional impact. Describe scenes, colors, or metaphors that align with the emotions you want to convey.

Example: When describing a moment of serenity in your composition, evoke images like "soft moonlight reflecting on a tranquil lake" to convey a peaceful atmosphere.

Experiment with Modalities

Tip: Experiment with different modalities (e.g., major, minor, modal scales) to evoke distinct emotional qualities. Each modality can contribute a unique flavor to your compositions.

Example: Utilize the Dorian mode for a composition that balances minor tonality with a slightly brighter, hopeful character.

Consider Cultural Influences

Tip: Be mindful of cultural influences that can shape emotional expressions. Explore how different cultures interpret and express emotions through music and incorporate these insights into your compositions.

Example: If you're drawing inspiration from flamenco music, experiment with the passionate and emotive qualities characteristic of this genre.

Explore Hybrid Emotions

Tip: Experiment with hybrid emotions by combining contrasting elements. This can result in compositions that convey complex and layered emotional experiences.

Example: Blend elements of excitement and nostalgia to create a composition that captures the bittersweet nature of a significant life event.

Invite Listener Interpretation

Tip: Allow room for listener interpretation. Craft compositions with emotional depth that listeners can relate to on a personal level, inviting them to find their own emotional connections.

Example: Create an instrumental piece with open-ended emotional cues, allowing listeners to project their own experiences and emotions onto the music.

Tips for Effective Emotional Exploration

Practice Emotional Awareness: Cultivate emotional awareness in your own experiences and surroundings to inform your compositions authentically.

Experiment with Metaphors: Use metaphors and analogies in your written reflections to articulate emotions in a way that resonates with readers.

Engage in Visualizations: Visualize the emotional landscapes you want to convey during your creative process, allowing the visualization to guide your musical choices.

By consciously exploring the emotional landscape of your musical ideas and expressing those emotions through words in your musical diary, you can create compositions that resonate on a deep emotional level. Experiment with various musical elements, draw inspiration from your own experiences, and use descriptive language to capture the nuanced emotions embedded in your compositions.

DOES THE IDEA HAVE A SPECIFIC THEME OR CONCEPT?

Consider whether the musical idea aligns with a specific theme, concept, or narrative. How can you articulate the underlying meaning or story behind the idea?

Attaching specific themes, concepts, or narratives to your ideas in your musical diary for guitar composition adds depth and meaning to your creative process.

Here are some themes, concepts, and narrative ideas, along with ways to articulate the underlying meaning or story behind each:

Nature and Landscapes

Concept: Use nature and landscapes as a theme, with each composition representing a different natural element or setting.

Articulation: Describe the imagery and emotions associated with each composition. Use words that evoke the sounds of the wind, the colors of a sunset, or the tranquility of a forest.

Example: *"A Wind's Lullaby": This composition captures the gentle rustling of leaves and the calming* *whispers of the wind through a melody that resonates with the serenity of nature.*

Journey and Exploration

Concept: Frame your compositions as a musical journey or exploration, allowing the narrative to unfold with each section.

Articulation: Describe the stages of the journey, the challenges faced, and the moments of discovery. Use words that convey movement, progression, and the evolving landscape.

Example: *"Quest for Harmony": This composition embarks on a musical quest, navigating through moments of tension and resolution, symbolizing the pursuit of inner harmony.*

Emotional Arcs

Concept: Craft compositions with distinct emotional arcs, taking listeners on a rollercoaster of feelings throughout the piece.

Articulation: Express the emotional shifts within the composition. Use words that describe the highs and lows, building tension, and moments of catharsis.

Example: *"Tears of Joy": This composition weaves through melancholic moments, building to a crescendo of joyous celebration, mirroring the emotional complexity of life's experiences.*

Cultural Fusion

Concept: Explore the fusion of different musical cultures, incorporating elements from diverse traditions into your compositions.

Articulation: Highlight the cultural influences and the blending of musical traditions. Use words that convey a rich tapestry of sounds and evoke the spirit of cross-cultural collaboration.

Example: *"Global Groove Medley": This composition seamlessly blends rhythmic patterns and melodic motifs from various cultures, creating a harmonious celebration of musical diversity.*

Time and Epochs

Concept: Base your compositions on different time periods or epochs, capturing the essence of historical eras through music.

Articulation: Describe the characteristics of the chosen era, and how the composition reflects the societal, cultural, or artistic elements of that time.

Example: *"Baroque Reverie": This composition draws inspiration from the Baroque era, incorporating ornate ornamentation and structured counterpoint to transport listeners to a bygone musical epoch.*

Human Emotions

Concept: Explore the rich spectrum of human emotions as the central theme for your compositions.

Articulation: Delve into the specific emotions represented in each piece. Use words that evoke empathy and connection, describing the emotional landscape you aim to convey.

Example: *"Solitude's Embrace": This composition explores the depths of solitude, weaving a musical tapestry that resonates with introspection, vulnerability, and inner contemplation.*

Fantasy and Mythology

Concept: Create compositions inspired by fantasy realms or mythological stories, allowing your imagination to conjure magical landscapes and characters.

Articulation: Describe the fantastical elements, characters, or settings within each composition. Use words that transport listeners to a mythical world.

Example: *"Elysian Echoes": This composition takes inspiration from Greek mythology, capturing the ethereal beauty of Elysium through enchanting melodies and mystical harmonies.*

Personal Narratives

Concept: Infuse your compositions with personal narratives, drawing on your own experiences, memories, or reflections.

Articulation: Share the personal stories behind each composition. Use words that convey authenticity, introspection, and a connection to your own life.

Example: *"Echoes of Home": This composition is a musical reflection on the memories and emotions* associated with your childhood home, weaving a nostalgic tapestry through melody and harmony.

Color Palette Inspirations

Concept: Draw inspiration from visual art and create compositions based on specific color palettes, translating visual aesthetics into musical expressions.

Articulation: Describe the colors and visual elements that inspired each composition. Use words that evoke the visual beauty and vibrancy of the chosen palette.

Example: *"Cerulean Serenade": This composition takes inspiration from the serene blue tones of a cerulean sky, translating the calming essence into a melodic serenade.*

Literary Themes

Concept: Explore literary themes or narratives, adapting stories, poems, or novels into musical compositions.

Articulation: Discuss the literary works that inspired each composition and how you interpreted the themes musically. Use words that connect the narrative elements to your musical choices.

Example: *"Shakespearean Sonata": This composition is inspired by the timeless themes of love and tragedy found in Shakespearean sonnets, translating the emotional depth into musical motifs.*

Cinematic Soundscapes

Concept: Craft compositions that evoke cinematic soundscapes, capturing the mood and atmosphere reminiscent of film scores.

Articulation: Describe the scenes or scenarios that the composition conjures. Use words that convey the cinematic elements, such as tension, drama, or sweeping landscapes.

Example: *"Epic Odyssey": This composition unfolds like the soundtrack to an epic journey, featuring dynamic shifts, climactic moments, and an overall cinematic grandeur.*

Philosophical Concepts

Concept: Base your compositions on philosophical concepts or ideas, translating abstract notions into tangible musical expressions.

Articulation: Discuss the philosophical themes or concepts behind each composition. Use words that convey the intellectual depth and contemplative nature of the chosen concept.

Example: *"Existential Elegy": This composition delves into existential themes, expressing the complex interplay between existence, meaning, and the human experience through musical exploration.*

Seasonal Inspirations

Concept: Explore the seasons as a theme for your compositions, capturing the unique characteristics and moods associated with each season.

Articulation: Describe the seasonal influences on the composition. Use words that evoke the sights, sounds, and emotions of a particular season.

Example: *"Winter Whispers": This composition captures the serene beauty of winter, with delicate melodies that evoke the hushed whispers of falling snow and the crisp air of a winter day.*

Abstract Concepts

Concept: Create compositions inspired by abstract concepts, such as dreams, memories, or metaphysical ideas.

Articulation: Discuss the abstract themes or concepts behind each composition. Use words that convey the intangible nature of the chosen concept.

Example: *"Astral Reverie": This composition explores the abstract realm of astral dreams, translating the ethereal and otherworldly qualities into musical expressions.*

Human Connections

Concept: Frame your compositions around the theme of human connections, exploring relationships, bonds, or shared experiences.

Articulation: Share the stories or emotions associated with human connections in each composition. Use words that convey the warmth, complexity, and intimacy of relationships.

Example: *"Kinship Serenade": This composition celebrates the bonds of kinship, weaving a musical* *serenade that reflects the shared history and emotional resonance within a close-knit group.*

Tips for Articulating Themes and Concepts

Use Descriptive Language: Employ vivid and descriptive language to articulate the theme or concept behind each composition.

Relate Personal Insights: Share personal insights or connections to the chosen themes, adding a layer of authenticity to your reflections.

Draw Visual Comparisons: Draw visual comparisons to enhance the imagery associated with your themes, allowing readers to envision the landscapes or scenarios your compositions evoke.

By attaching specific themes, concepts, or narratives to your musical ideas and articulating the underlying meaning or story behind each, you create a rich and immersive experience for both yourself and your audience. Experiment with these ideas, allowing your musical diary to serve as a canvas for exploring a diverse range of themes and expressing the depth of your creative vision.

WHAT CHORD PROGRESSIONS AM I USING?

Document the chord progressions involved in the musical idea. Note the specific chords, their voicings, and any modulations or transitions you're experimenting with.

Documenting chord progressions in your musical diary for guitar composition is essential for preserving your creative ideas and facilitating future exploration and development.

Let's learn how to effectively document chord progressions, including noting specific chords, their voicings, and any modulations or transitions you're experimenting with.

Use Standard Chord Notation

Method: Write down the chord progressions using standard chord notation. Use chord symbols such as C, G, Dm, Am, etc.

Example:
```
| C  | G  | Am  | F  |
| Dm | G  | Em  | F  |
```

Include Chord Voicings

Method: Specify the voicings of the chords by indicating the fret numbers and strings for each chord. This provides a detailed reference for reproducing the exact sound.

Example:
```
| C  | G  | Am7  | Fmaj7  |
| Dm7 | G  | Em   | Fmaj7  |
```

In this example, the specific voicings for Am7 and Fmaj7 are included, providing clarity on the chord shapes used.

Note Modulations or Key Changes

Method: If you experiment with modulations or key changes, clearly indicate when and how these transitions occur. Note the key signature and chords involved in the modulation.

Example:
```
|C  |G  |Am  |F  |
|Dm  |G  |C  |E7  |
|Am  |D  |G  |G#dim  |
```

In this example, there's a modulation from the key of C to the key of G, and then to the key of D, accompanied by appropriate chord changes.

Describe Strumming or Picking Patterns

Method: Include information about strumming or picking patterns if they are integral to the chord progression. Use symbols or brief descriptions to convey the desired rhythm.

Example:
```
|C  |G  |Am  |F  |
|Dm  |G  |Em  |F  |
Strumming pattern: DUDU–UDUD for each chord
```

Annotate Dynamic Changes

Method: Annotate dynamic changes, indicating whether certain chords should be played softly (piano) or loudly (forte). Use symbols like 'p' and 'f' for dynamics.

Example:
```
|C  |G  |Am  |F  |
|Dm  |G  |Em  |F  |
Dynamic change: Play the Fmaj7 chord in the second chorus with more intensity (forte).
```

Record Tempo and Time Signature

Method: Include the tempo and time signature information at the beginning of your chord progressions. This helps maintain consistency and provides a reference for future performances.

Example:
```
Tempo: 120 BPM
Time Signature: 4/4
```

Create Section Labels

Method: Divide your composition into sections (verse, chorus, bridge, etc.) and label each section. This makes it easier to navigate and organize your chord progressions.

Example:
```
Verse 1:
```

```
|C  |G  |Am  |F  |
```
Chorus:
```
|Dm  |G  |Em  |F  |
```

Utilize Color-Coding or Symbols

Method: Consider using color-coding or symbols to visually represent specific aspects of your chord progressions, such as highlighting key changes or marking sections with distinct characteristics.
Example:
```

|C  |G  |Am  |F  |
|Dm  |G  |Em  |F  |
(!) Key change to G major from this point forward.
```

Date and Contextual Notes

Method: Include the date of your entry and any contextual notes about the inspiration or mood behind the chord progressions. This provides valuable context when revisiting your ideas.
Example:
Date: February 17, 2024
Context: Experimenting with a nostalgic chord progression inspired by a rainy afternoon.

Use Software or Apps for Digital Documentation

Method: Consider using digital tools, such as music notation software or chord chart apps, for more organized and easily shareable documentation.

Example: Applications like Guitar Pro, MuseScore, or Chordify allow you to create, edit, and share chord progressions digitally.

By following these methods, you can ensure that your chord progressions are accurately documented in your musical diary, providing a comprehensive reference for future exploration and development of your guitar compositions.

ARE THERE UNIQUE RHYTHMIC PATTERNS OR TECHNIQUES?

Identify any distinctive rhythmic patterns or guitar techniques employed in the idea. This could include fingerpicking styles, strumming patterns, or percussive elements.

Identifying distinctive rhythmic patterns and guitar techniques in your musical diary for guitar composition is crucial for capturing the essence of your ideas and facilitating the reproduction of those patterns during future performances or developments.

Listen Closely

Method: Play through your musical idea and listen closely to the rhythmic nuances and techniques employed. Pay attention to variations in strumming, picking patterns, and any percussive elements.

Analyze Strumming Patterns

Method: Identify the strumming pattern used in your composition. This could involve downstrokes, upstrokes, or a combination of both. Note any emphasis on specific beats.

Example:
```

Strumming Pattern: DDUUDU (Down-Down-Up-Up-Down-Up)
```

Recognize Fingerpicking Styles

Method: If fingerpicking is employed, identify the specific fingerpicking style. This could include classical fingerstyle, Travis picking, or fingerstyle patterns using individual fingers.

Example:
```

Fingerpicking Style: Travis Picking (Thumb on bass notes, index and middle fingers on melody and harmony)
```

Document Percussive Elements:

Method: If your composition incorporates percussive elements such as tapping, slapping, or using the guitar body as a percussion instrument, document these techniques.

Example:
```

Percussive Element: Light body percussion on beats 2 and 4 using palm muting.
```

Note Dynamics and Accentuations

Method: Pay attention to dynamic variations and accentuations. Identify where the intensity increases or decreases and any specific accents on certain beats or notes.

Example:
```

Dynamics: Gradual build-up in intensity during the chorus with accentuated downstrokes on the first beat of each measure.
```

Identify Palm Muting or Harmonics

Method: If you employ palm muting or harmonics, make a note of these techniques. Palm muting can create a percussive effect, while harmonics add a distinctive tone.

Example:
```

Technique: Palm muting during the verses for a subdued effect. Harmonics on the 12th fret in the bridge.
```

Recognize Hybrid Picking

Method: If you use a combination of picking and fingerpicking (hybrid picking), document where and how this technique is applied.

Example:

```

Technique: Hybrid picking on the bridge section, with a pick used for bass notes and fingers for melody notes.

```

Document Slides, Bends, and Vibrato

Method: Note any slides, bends, or vibrato applied to individual notes. These techniques can add expressiveness and character to your composition.

Example:

```

Technique: Vibrato applied to sustained notes in the chorus. Slides on the G string during the instrumental break.

```


Use Symbols for Notation

Method: Consider using symbols or abbreviations to represent different techniques. For example, 'P' for palm muting, 'H' for hammer-ons, or 'T' for tapping.

Example:

```

Symbol Notation: Pm (Palm Muting), Ho (Hammer-ons), Ta (Tapping)

```

Include Tempo and Feel Descriptors

Method: Note the tempo and describe the overall feel of the rhythmic patterns. Is it upbeat, laid-back, syncopated, or steady?

Example:
```

Tempo: 120 BPM
Feel: Upbeat with a syncopated strumming
pattern in the chorus.
```

Record Specific Techniques

Method: Create a separate section in your musical diary dedicated to specific techniques used in your composition. List each technique along with the corresponding section of the composition.

Example:
```

Techniques Used:
Fingerstyle pattern in Verse 1
Slap-and-pop technique in Bridge
Harmonics in Intro
```

Date and Contextual Notes

Method: Include the date of your entry and any contextual notes about the inspiration or mood behind the rhythmic patterns and techniques. This provides valuable context when revisiting your ideas.

Example:
```

Date: February 17, 2024
Context: Exploring percussive fingerstyle techniques inspired by Flamenco rhythms.
```

```
```

By following these steps and providing detailed descriptions of the rhythmic patterns, fingerpicking styles, strumming patterns, and percussive elements, you create a comprehensive reference in your musical diary. This documentation not only aids in reproducing your compositions but also serves as a valuable resource for future experimentation and development of your guitar ideas.

HOW WOULD YOU DESCRIBE THE DYNAMICS OF THE IDEA?

Describe the dynamics of the musical idea. Does it have moments of tension and release? How do volume changes contribute to the overall expression?

Describing the dynamics of your musical idea in your musical diary for guitar composition involves capturing the variations in volume, intensity, and expressiveness throughout the composition. Dynamics play a crucial role in shaping the emotional impact and overall feel of your music.

Here's a guide on how to effectively describe the dynamics of your musical idea:

Understand Dynamic Terms

Method: Familiarize yourself with dynamic terms used in music notation, such as piano (soft), forte (loud), mezzo piano (moderately soft), mezzo forte (moderately loud), crescendo (gradually getting louder), and decrescendo (gradually getting softer).

Document Gradual Changes

Method: Note any gradual changes in volume or intensity. Describe how the dynamics evolve from one section to another, creating a sense of ebb and flow.

Example:
```

Dynamics: The piece starts with a gentle piano introduction, gradually building to a powerful forte in the chorus before tapering off in the final verse.
```

Specify Intensity Levels

Method: Use descriptive language to specify the intensity levels at different points in your composition. Mention when the music should be played with passion, delicacy, or vigor.
Example:
```

Dynamics: The bridge section calls for a heightened intensity, played with a fervent forte, emphasizing the emotional climax of the composition.
```

Note Articulation Techniques

Method: Describe any articulation techniques that contribute to the dynamics, such as staccato (short and detached) or legato (smooth and connected). These techniques can influence the perceived volume and energy.

Example:
```

Dynamics: The verses feature a legato phrasing, creating a seamless flow, while the chorus incorporates staccato strumming for added emphasis and punch.
```

Highlight Dynamic Contrasts

Method: Emphasize dynamic contrasts between different sections or phrases. Note when the music transitions from soft to loud or vice versa, creating impactful moments.

Example:
```

Dynamics: The transition from the subdued verse to the powerful chorus creates a stark dynamic contrast, enhancing the emotional impact of the composition.
```

Use Symbols for Notation

Method: Consider using symbols or abbreviations to represent specific dynamics. For instance, 'p' for piano, 'f' for forte, '<' for a gradual decrease, and '>' for a gradual increase.

Example:
```
```

Dynamics: The instrumental break features a crescendo (<) leading into a thunderous forte (f) chord progression.
```

## Describe Dynamic Surprises

Method: Note any unexpected or surprising dynamic changes that add excitement or drama to your composition. These can include sudden jumps in volume or abrupt shifts in intensity.

**Example**:
```

Dynamics: A sudden piano interlude in the midst of a forte section adds an element of surprise, creating a moment of introspection before the intensity resumes.
```

## Consider Phrasing and Expression

**Method**: Consider how phrasing and expression contribute to the dynamics. Describe how variations in picking strength, strumming intensity, or note articulation affect the overall dynamic range.

**Example**:
```

Dynamics: The use of subtle fingerpicking in the verses enhances the intimate nature of the composition, while powerful strumming in the chorus adds dynamic intensity.
```

## Document Tempo Changes
```

Method: Note any changes in tempo that may affect the perceived dynamics. Faster tempos can contribute to a sense of urgency, while slower tempos may create a more contemplative feel.

Example:
```

Dynamics: The tempo increases during the instrumental solo, intensifying the overall energy and contributing to a dynamic shift in the composition.
```

Include Contextual Notes

Method: Provide contextual notes about the emotions or themes associated with specific dynamic changes. This helps convey the intended mood or atmosphere of your musical idea.

Example:
```

Dynamics: The dynamic swells in the outro mirror the emotional intensity of bidding farewell, creating a poignant and memorable conclusion to the composition.
```

Record Specific Techniques

Method: Create a separate section in your musical diary dedicated to specific dynamic techniques used in your composition. List each technique along with the corresponding section of the composition.

Example:
```

Dynamic Techniques Used:
Gradual crescendo in the pre-chorus
Staccato strumming in the bridge
```

Date and Contextual Notes

Method: Include the date of your entry and any contextual notes about the inspiration or mood behind the dynamic choices. This provides valuable context when revisiting your ideas.

Example:
```

Date: February 17, 2024
Context: Experimenting with dynamic contrasts to convey the emotional journey of resilience and triumph.
```

By describing the dynamics in detail, you create a comprehensive reference in your musical diary that captures the nuances and expressive qualities of your composition. This documentation not only helps in reproducing your musical ideas but also serves as a valuable resource for future interpretations and refinements of your guitar compositions.

ARE THERE NOTABLE MELODIC ELEMENTS?

Document the melodic elements of your idea. Identify specific melodies, motifs, or memorable phrases that stand out.

Documenting the melodic elements of your musical idea in your diary for guitar composition is crucial for preserving the distinctive and memorable aspects of your composition.

Let's document melodic elements, including identifying specific melodies, motifs, or memorable phrases:

Identify Key Melodies

Method: Pinpoint the primary melodies that form the backbone of your composition. These are the central themes or motifs that are likely to be repeated or developed throughout the piece.

Example:
```

Key Melody: The opening arpeggio pattern serves as the foundational melody, introducing the main musical theme of the composition.
```

Note Motifs and Repetition

Method: Identify motifs—short, recurring musical ideas—that contribute to the overall melodic structure. Note instances of repetition or variations on these motifs.

Example:
```

Motif: The ascending three-note motif in the chorus is repeated and varied, creating a sense of continuity and cohesion in the melodic progression.
```

```

### Document Memorable Phrases

**Method**: Highlight specific melodic phrases that stand out as memorable or distinctive. These phrases often contribute to the emotional impact or catchiness of your composition.
**Example**:
```

Memorable Phrase: The soaring guitar solo in the bridge features a melodic phrase that adds a dramatic and memorable element to the overall composition.
```

### Describe Melodic Contours

**Method**: Use descriptive language to characterize the melodic contours. Is the melody rising, falling, undulating, or maintaining a static pitch? This helps convey the overall shape of the melodic line.
**Example**:
```

Melodic Contour: The verse melody follows a gentle rise and fall, creating a soothing and reflective quality in contrast to the dynamic chorus.
```

### Identify Climactic Moments

**Method**: Note any climactic moments or peak points in the melody. These are instances where the melodic
```

intensity or range reaches a notable high, contributing to the emotional impact.
   Example:
```

Climactic Moment: The melody reaches its climactic peak during the final chorus, accentuating the emotional crescendo of the composition.
```

Record Intervallic Relationships

   Method: Document the intervals—distances between pitches—in your melodies. This information provides insights into the overall character and movement of the melodic lines.
   Example:
```

Intervallic Relationships: The chorus melody features wide intervals, creating a sense of expansiveness and grandeur in the overall melodic structure.
```

Include Chord Ties and Harmonic Interplay

   Method: Describe how the melodies interact with the underlying chords or harmonic progressions. Note instances where the melody creates tension, resolution, or harmonic embellishments.
   Example:
```
```

Chord Ties: The melody in the pre-chorus creates harmonic tension by emphasizing a dissonant note, leading to a satisfying resolution in the subsequent chorus.
```

## Document Variations and Developments

**Method**: If your composition features variations or developments of melodic themes, document these changes. Note how the melodies evolve over the course of the composition.

**Example**:
```

Melodic Development: The initial motif introduced in the introduction undergoes a series of variations and developments, adding complexity and interest to the melody.
```

## Use Musical Notation or Tablature

**Method**: If you're comfortable with musical notation or tablature, consider using these formats to document specific melodic elements. This provides a more detailed and accurate representation of the melodies.

**Example**:
```

```
|-------------------|-------------------|
|-------------------|-------------------|
|-------7--9--7---|-------7--9--10-|
|---9-------------|---9-------------|
```

```
|- - - - - - - - - - - - - - - -|- - - - - - - - - - - - - - - -|
|- - - - - - - - - - - - - - - -|- - - - - - - - - - - - - - - -|
```
```

### *Include Tempo and Articulation*

**Method**: Describe how the tempo and articulation contribute to the melodic elements. Note any changes in tempo that affect the perceived speed of the melodies and describe how legato, staccato, or other articulations influence the melodic feel.

**Example**:
```

Tempo: The uptempo pace in the instrumental section enhances the energetic quality of the melody. Legato phrasing in the verses creates a smooth and connected feel.
```

### *Date and Contextual Notes*

**Method**: Include the date of your entry and any contextual notes about the inspiration or mood behind the melodic elements. This provides valuable context when revisiting your ideas.

**Example**:
```

Date: February 17, 2024
Context: Exploring melodic motifs inspired by the beauty of nature and the changing seasons.
```

### *Record Specific Techniques*
```

Method: Create a separate section in your musical diary dedicated to specific techniques used in your melodic elements. List each technique along with the corresponding section of the composition.

Example:
```

Melodic Techniques Used:
Slide between notes in the chorus melody
Hammer-ons and pull-offs in the instrumental break
```

By following these steps and providing detailed descriptions of specific melodies, motifs, or memorable phrases, you create a comprehensive reference in your musical diary that captures the melodic essence of your composition. This documentation not only aids in reproducing your musical ideas but also serves as a valuable resource for future exploration and development of your guitar compositions.

DOES THE IDEA FEATURE UNCONVENTIONAL TUNINGS OR CAPO POSITIONS?

If you're experimenting with unconventional tunings or capo positions, record these details. How do these choices contribute to the unique character of the idea?

Exploring unconventional tunings and capo positions can open up new creative possibilities in guitar composition. Documenting these elements in your musical diary is essential for reproducing or developing your compositions later.

Here are some unconventional tunings and capo positions:

Unconventional Tunings

Open D Minor (DADFAD):
Lowering the third and fifth strings to create an open D minor chord.
Documenting in Diary:
```

Tuning: DADFAD (Open D Minor)
```

DADGAD with a Drop C (C#) Bass (C#ADGAD):
Retaining the DADGAD structure while dropping the low E string to C# for added depth.
Documenting in Diary:
```

Tuning: C#ADGAD (DADGAD with Drop C# Bass)
```

Open C6 (CACGCE):
Creating a major sixth chord by tuning strings to C, A, C, G, C, E.
Documenting in Diary:
```

Tuning: CACGCE (Open C6)
```

Dropped D with High A (DADF#AA):

Keeping the low E string dropped to D and raising the high E string to A.

Documenting in Diary:

```

Tuning: DADF#AA (Dropped D with High A)
```


Open G Major (DGDGBD):
Creating an open G major chord by tuning strings accordingly.

Documenting in Diary:

```

Tuning: DGDGBD (Open G Major)
```


Capo Positions

Capo on the 5th Fret (Standard Tuning):
Shifting the pitch up by a fourth.

Documenting in Diary:

```

Capo Position: 5th Fret (Standard Tuning)
```


Capo on the 7th Fret (Drop D Tuning):
Applying a capo to Drop D tuning.

Documenting in Diary:

```

Capo Position: 7th Fret (Drop D Tuning)
```


Partial Capo on the 2nd Fret (EADGBE):

Using a partial capo to alter the tuning of specific strings while keeping the standard tuning intact.

Documenting in Diary:
```

Capo Position: Partial on 2nd Fret (EADGBE)
```


Capo Across the 3rd–5th Frets (Alternate Tuning):
Employing a capo across multiple frets to create an alternate tuning effect.

Documenting in Diary:
```

Capo Position: 3rd–5th Frets (Alternate Tuning)
```


Tips for Documenting in Your Musical Diary

Clearly Specify Tunings and Capo Positions: Clearly state the unconventional tuning or capo position used in your composition. Provide details on which strings are adjusted and any specific instructions for capo placement.

Include Musical Notation or Chord Diagrams: If possible, include musical notation or chord diagrams to visually represent the unconventional tuning or capo position. This can make it easier to understand and reproduce your compositions.

Describe the Creative Intention: Include notes about why you chose a particular tuning or capo position. Describe the creative intention behind these choices and how they contribute to the overall mood or atmosphere of your composition.

Record Any Adjustments or Variations: If you make adjustments or variations within the unconventional tuning or capo position, document these changes in your diary. Note any specific alterations to the standard tuning or capo placement.

Provide Contextual Information: Include contextual information about when and why you decided to experiment with unconventional tunings or capo positions. This can help you recall the inspiration or mood behind your creative choices.

Example Entry in Your Musical Diary

```

*Date:* February 17, 2024

*Composition:* "Ethereal Reverie"

*Tuning:* C#ADGAD (DADGAD with Drop C# Bass)

*Capo Position:* 5th Fret (Standard Tuning)

*Creative Intention:* Explored the resonant tones of the DADGAD tuning with a drop C# bass note for a dreamlike quality. Applied a capo on the 5th fret to elevate the tonal range and enhance the ethereal atmosphere.

*Adjustments/Variations:* Emphasized the higher register with intricate fingerpicking patterns. Experimented with chord voicings to complement the capo position.
```

<u>Contextual Notes:</u> Inspired by a celestial night sky, aimed to capture the otherworldly feeling through unconventional tunings and capo placements.

By thoroughly documenting your use of unconventional tunings and capo positions in your musical diary, you create a comprehensive reference that captures the unique elements of your compositions. This information is invaluable for future performances, adaptations, or expansions of your guitar pieces.

What Is the Overall Mood or Atmosphere of the Idea?

Reflect on the overall mood or atmosphere created by the musical idea. How would you describe the sonic landscape you're aiming to achieve?

Describing the mood, atmosphere, and sonic landscape of your guitar composition in your musical diary is essential for conveying the emotional and tonal qualities you intend to capture.

Here are some moods and atmospheres to consider as you articulate the sonic landscape you're aiming to achieve:

Reflective and Nostalgic

Description: The composition evokes a sense of introspection and longing, reminiscent of fond memories or bittersweet moments.

Example:
```

Mood: Reflective and Nostalgic
```

Sonic Landscape: The gentle arpeggios and warm, mellow tones create a sonic landscape that transports the listener to a bygone era, filled with sentimental reflections.
```

## Energetic and Upbeat

**Description**: The music exudes energy, enthusiasm, and a lively tempo, creating an uplifting and dynamic sonic experience.

**Example**:
```

Mood: Energetic and Upbeat
Sonic Landscape: The driving rhythm, brisk strumming patterns, and upbeat chord progressions establish a sonic landscape filled with vitality and positivity.
```

## Mysterious and Enigmatic

**Description**: The composition carries an air of mystery and intrigue, with unconventional harmonies and atmospheric elements.

**Example**:
```

Mood: Mysterious and Enigmatic
Sonic Landscape: Haunting melodies, ethereal reverb, and dissonant chords contribute to a sonic landscape that feels enigmatic, inviting the listener into a mysterious realm.
```
```

Gentle and Soothing

Description: The music is characterized by soft dynamics, gentle fingerpicking, and a calming melody, creating a soothing and tranquil atmosphere.
Example:
```

Mood: Gentle and Soothing
Sonic Landscape: The delicate interplay of fingerpicked notes, subtle harmonics, and a warm tone contribute to a sonic landscape that is tender and comforting.
```

Epic and Cinematic

Description: The composition aims to evoke grandeur and cinematic scope, with expansive chords, dynamic swells, and powerful melodic themes.
Example:
```

Mood: Epic and Cinematic
Sonic Landscape: Majestic chord progressions, sweeping arpeggios, and orchestral elements create a sonic landscape that feels larger-than-life, akin to a cinematic score.
```

Intimate and Personal

Description: The music conveys a sense of intimacy and personal connection, with emotive melodies and vulnerable chord progressions.
Example:
```

Mood: Intimate and Personal
Sonic Landscape: Close-miked acoustic guitar, heartfelt lyrics, and nuanced dynamics contribute to a sonic landscape that feels deeply personal and emotionally resonant.
```

Dreamy and Ethereal

Description: The composition creates an otherworldly atmosphere, with dreamlike textures, ambient effects, and a sense of weightlessness.
Example:
```

Mood: Dreamy and Ethereal
Sonic Landscape: Delay-soaked guitar, harmonic swells, and atmospheric effects create a sonic landscape that transports the listener to a dreamy and otherworldly realm.
```

Dark and Brooding

Description: The music explores darker tones, with minor chords, dissonant intervals, and a sense of tension and foreboding.
Example:

```

Mood: Dark and Brooding
Sonic Landscape: Low, rumbling bass notes, distorted guitar tones, and haunting melodies contribute to a sonic landscape that feels ominous and mysterious.
```

Playful and Quirky

Description: The composition exudes a sense of playfulness and whimsy, with unconventional chord progressions, unexpected rhythmic elements, and a lighthearted feel.
Example:
```

Mood: Playful and Quirky
Sonic Landscape: Jazzy chords, percussive slaps, and upbeat, whimsical melodies create a sonic landscape that is playful and filled with quirky charm.
```

Serene and Meditative

Description: The music induces a sense of calmness and meditation, with slow tempos, open chords, and spacious arrangements.
Example:
```

Mood: Serene and Meditative
Sonic Landscape: Extended sustains, ambient textures, and minimalistic arrangements contribute
```

to a sonic landscape that invites contemplation and tranquility.
```

## Dynamic and Explosive

**Description**: The composition features sudden bursts of intensity, dynamic contrasts, and explosive moments that add excitement and drama.
**Example**:
```

Mood: Dynamic and Explosive
Sonic Landscape: Percussive attacks, sharp staccato phrases, and powerful chord strums create a sonic landscape that is dynamically charged and impactful.
```

## Folksy and Earthy

**Description**: The music carries a down-to-earth, folksy charm with acoustic textures, open chords, and a connection to nature.

**Example**:
```

Mood: Folksy and Earthy
Sonic Landscape: Fingerpicked acoustic guitar, organic percussion, and rustic tonalities contribute to a sonic landscape that feels grounded and connected to the earth.
```

## How to Document in Your Musical Diary
```

Use Descriptive Language: Employ descriptive language to articulate the mood and atmosphere you aim to achieve. Consider adjectives such as "ethereal," "intimate," "brooding," or "uplifting."

Specify Sonic Elements: Describe specific sonic elements, such as chord progressions, tonal characteristics, effects, and dynamic changes, that contribute to the overall sonic landscape.

Note Inspirations: Include any sources of inspiration or references that influence the mood and sonic landscape you're aiming for. This provides additional context for your creative process.

Use Analogies: Draw analogies or comparisons to non-musical elements (nature, emotions, colors) to further convey the intended mood and atmosphere.

Experiment with Metaphors: Experiment with metaphors to describe the sonic qualities, comparing the music to visual or sensory experiences that capture the essence of your composition.

Include Visual or Imaginary References: If applicable, reference visual or imaginary landscapes that align with the sonic qualities you're aiming for. This helps create a vivid image of the intended atmosphere.

Utilize Musical Notation: If you're comfortable with musical notation, you can include simple chord progressions, melodic outlines, or even tablature to provide a more visual representation of the sonic landscape.

Date and Contextual Notes: As always, include the date of your entry and any contextual notes about your mindset, emotions, or external factors influencing the creation of the mood and atmosphere.

By effectively describing the mood, atmosphere, and sonic landscape, you create a vivid and immersive reference in your musical diary. This documentation not only helps in conveying your creative vision but also serves as a valuable guide for future exploration and refinement of your guitar compositions.

DOES THE IDEA HAVE A CLEAR STRUCTURE OR FORM?

Consider the structure or form of the musical idea. Does it follow a traditional song structure, or are you exploring a more unconventional arrangement?

Documenting the structure or form of your guitar composition in your musical diary is crucial for understanding the organization and flow of your musical ideas. Various traditional and unconventional structures can shape a composition.

Traditional Song Structures

Verse-Chorus-Verse (VCV): A common and widely used structure featuring verses and choruses. Verses usually convey the narrative, while choruses provide a repeated, catchy refrain.

Example:
```

Structure: VCV
Verse 1
Chorus
```

```
Verse 2
Chorus
Bridge
Chorus (Repeat)
```

Verse-Pre-Chorus-Chorus (VPC): Similar to VCV but includes a pre-chorus section that builds tension before leading into the chorus.

Example:
```
Structure: VPC
Verse 1
Pre-Chorus
Chorus
Verse 2
Pre-Chorus
Chorus (Repeat)
```

AABA (32-Bar Form): A classic song form featuring two contrasting sections (A and B) followed by a return to the initial section (A).

Example:
```
Structure: AABA
Section A
Section A
Section B
Section A
```

Rondo Form (ABACA): A recurring structure where a main theme (A) alternates with contrasting sections (B, C, etc.) before returning to the main theme.

Example:
```

Structure: ABACA
Section A
Section B
Section A
Section C
Section A
```


Verse-Verse-Bridge-Verse (VVBV): An alternative structure with multiple verses, a bridge providing contrast, and a return to the verse.

Example:
```

Structure: VVBV
Verse 1
Verse 2
Bridge
Verse 3
```

Unconventional Arrangements

Through-Composed: A structure where each section of the composition is unique, without significant repetition. It evolves continuously.

Example:
```
```

```
Structure: Through-Composed
Intro
Section 1
Section 2
Section 3
Outro
```

Circular Form: The composition loops back to the beginning without a clear endpoint, creating a continuous, cyclical feel.

Example:

```
Structure: Circular Form
Section 1
Section 2
Section 3
(Loop back to Section 1)
```

Nonlinear Structure: Sections are arranged in a non-sequential order, offering flexibility and unexpected transitions.

Example:

```
Structure: Nonlinear
Section C
Section A
Section B
```

Suite or Medley: Multiple distinct sections or themes are connected within a larger composition.

Example:

```

Structure: Suite
Theme 1
Theme 2
Theme 3
```


Free Form: The composition lacks a predetermined structure, allowing for spontaneous changes and improvisation.

Example:

```

Structure: Free Form
(No fixed sections, open to improvisation)
```

Collage Structure: Various contrasting elements or musical fragments are juxtaposed without a traditional narrative.

Example:

```

Structure: Collage
Fragment A
Fragment B
Fragment C
```

How to Document in Your Musical Diary

Use Section Labels: Clearly label each section of your composition, such as Verse, Chorus, Bridge, etc.

Indicate Repeats: Note where sections are repeated or if there's a specific order to follow.

Include Time Markers: Specify approximate timestamps for each section or major change to help with pacing.

Describe Transitions: Document how transitions between sections are executed, whether through modulation, dynamics, or thematic connections.

Note Dynamics and Intensity: Describe the dynamic changes or intensity levels in each section, contributing to the overall structure.

Include Lyrics or Themes: If applicable, incorporate lyrics or thematic elements associated with each section.

Consider Diagrams or Visuals: Use diagrams or visual representations, such as flowcharts, to illustrate the structural flow of your composition.

Date and Contextual Notes: Include the date of your entry and any contextual notes about your mindset, emotions, or external factors influencing the structure of your composition.

By documenting the structure or form in your musical diary, you create a valuable roadmap for your composition, aiding in rehearsals, performances, or future developments. This information also serves as a reference point for analyzing and refining your creative decisions in the context of the overall composition.

HAVE YOU EXPERIMENTED WITH INSTRUMENTATION BEYOND GUITAR?

If you've incorporated additional instruments or effects, document these choices. How do these elements enhance the overall texture of the idea?

Experimenting with additional instrumentation beyond the guitar can significantly enhance the overall texture and depth of your composition. Whether incorporating other instruments or experimenting with unconventional sounds, documenting these choices in your musical diary is essential for reference and future development.

Here are some ways to document experimenting with instrumentation beyond guitar and adding these elements in your musical diary:

Selecting Additional Instruments

Experimentation: Explore various instruments that complement the guitar and contribute to the desired mood or atmosphere. Consider traditional options (piano, percussion, strings) or unconventional choices (synthesizers, ethnic instruments, sound effects).

Example:

```
Additional Instruments:
Cello for rich, emotive melodies
Hand percussion for rhythmic texture
Synthesizer for atmospheric effects
```

Arranging and Orchestrating

Layering: Experiment with layering different instruments to create a rich sonic tapestry. Consider the roles each instrument plays—melody, harmony, rhythm, or texture.

Example:
```

Arrangement:
Guitar: Main melody and chords
Cello: Counterpoint and emotive harmonies
Percussion: Rhythmic accents and textures
Synthesizer: Ambient pads and atmospheric effects
```

Effect Processing

Sound Design: Explore the use of effects and processing to modify the timbre of instruments. This can include reverb, delay, modulation, or other effects to create unique sonic textures.

Example:
```

Effect Processing:
Cello with subtle reverb for a spacious feel
Synthesizer with delay for ethereal textures
Percussion with panning and modulation for spatial movement
```

Dynamic Considerations

Dynamic Contrast: Experiment with dynamic variations between instruments to create moments of tension and release. Consider how different instruments contribute to the overall dynamic range.

Example:
```

Dynamic Considerations:
Cello builds intensity in the chorus
Synthesizer swells for transitions between sections
Percussion provides dynamic accents in key moments
```

Documenting in Your Musical Diary

Instrumentation List: Create a list of additional instruments you plan to incorporate. Include traditional and unconventional choices.

Arrangement Notes: Document the specific roles each instrument plays in the arrangement. This could include melody, harmony, rhythm, or texture.

Effect Settings: Note the settings of any effects or processing applied to each instrument. This ensures consistency during recording or future performances.

Dynamic Plan: Describe how the dynamics of each instrument contribute to the overall dynamic flow of the composition. Note any planned crescendos, decrescendos, or dynamic contrasts.

Interaction Between Instruments: Document how different instruments interact with each other. Describe moments of collaboration, call-and-response, or interplay.

Visual Representations: Use diagrams or visual representations to illustrate the arrangement and interaction of instruments. This can be particularly helpful for complex compositions.

Date and Contextual Notes: Include the date of your entry and any contextual notes about your mindset, emotions, or external factors influencing your choices regarding instrumentation.

Example Entry:
```

*Date: February 17, 2024*
*Instrumentation Experimentation:*
*Additional Instruments:*
*Cello for rich, emotive melodies*
*Hand percussion for rhythmic texture*
*Synthesizer for atmospheric effects*
*Arrangement:*
*Guitar: Main melody and chords*
*Cello: Counterpoint and emotive harmonies*
*Percussion: Rhythmic accents and textures*
*Synthesizer: Ambient pads and atmospheric effects*
*Effect Processing:*
*Cello with subtle reverb for a spacious feel*
*Synthesizer with delay for ethereal textures*
*Percussion with panning and modulation for spatial movement*
*Dynamic Considerations:*
*Cello builds intensity in the chorus*
*Synthesizer swells for transitions between sections*
*Percussion provides dynamic accents in key moments*
*Visual Representation:*
*[Include a simple diagram illustrating the arrangement]*
*Notes:*
*Experimenting with the combination of cello and synthesizer to create a dreamy, atmospheric quality.*
```

Percussion adds a rhythmic foundation and energy to the composition. Excited to see how these elements interact during the recording process.
```

By documenting your experimentation with additional instrumentation, you create a comprehensive reference in your musical diary. This information not only helps in the rehearsal and recording stages but also serves as a valuable resource for future exploration and refinement of your guitar compositions.

## IS THERE A SPECIFIC TEMPO OR FEEL?

Note the tempo and feel of the idea. Is it fast or slow? Does it have a specific rhythmic feel, such as a shuffle, swing, or straight groove?

Tempos in guitar compositions can vary widely, and the choice of tempo plays a significant role in shaping the overall feel and mood of a piece.

Here are some common tempos and how to document specific rhythmic feels such as a shuffle, swing, or straight groove in your musical diary:

### Common Tempos

Largo (40–60 BPM): Very slow and broad.
Adagio (66–76 BPM): Slow and stately.
Andante (76–108 BPM): At a walking pace.
Moderato (108–120 BPM): At a moderate tempo.
Allegro (120–168 BPM): Fast, cheerful.
Presto (168–200 BPM): Very fast.
```

Prestissimo (over 200 BPM): As fast as possible.

Shuffle Feel

Description: A triplet-based feel with a distinctive emphasis on the first and third beats of each triplet.
Example:
```

Tempo: 90 BPM
Rhythmic Feel: Shuffle
(Main groove with triplet subdivision)
```

Swing Feel

Description: A rhythmic feel where eighth notes are played with a long-short or "swing" pattern.
Example:
```

Tempo: 120 BPM
Rhythmic Feel: Swing
(Eighth notes played with a swung feel)
```

Straight Groove

Description: A straightforward, evenly divided rhythmic feel without swing or shuffle.
Example:
```

Tempo: 140 BPM
Rhythmic Feel: Straight
(Even eighth notes without swing or shuffle)
```

```
```

Combining Tempos and Feels

Upbeat Shuffle: A shuffle feel at a moderate to fast tempo, conveying an energetic and lively atmosphere.
Example:
```
```

Tempo: 160 BPM
Rhythmic Feel: Upbeat Shuffle
(Energetic shuffle feel with a faster tempo)
```
```

Slow Swing Ballad: A swing feel at a slow tempo, often used in ballads to create a relaxed and expressive mood.
Example:
```
```

Tempo: 80 BPM
Rhythmic Feel: Slow Swing Ballad
(Slow swing feel for a laid-back ballad)
```
```

Funky Straight Groove: A straight groove with a funky and syncopated feel, often emphasizing off-beats.
Example:
```
```

Tempo: 100 BPM
Rhythmic Feel: Funky Straight Groove
(Syncopated and funky straight groove)
```
```

Documenting in Your Musical Diary

Tempo Indication: Clearly specify the tempo of your composition, using BPM (Beats Per Minute).

Rhythmic Feel Description: Include a brief description of the desired rhythmic feel, such as shuffle, swing, or straight.

Notation or Tablature: If you're comfortable with notation or tablature, use it to document specific rhythmic patterns or grooves.

Metronome Markings: Note any specific metronome markings that align with the tempo and feel you want to achieve.

Visual Representations: Utilize visual representations, such as rhythmic notation or charts, to illustrate the rhythmic feel.

Contextual Notes: Include any contextual notes about the mood or emotions you aim to convey through the chosen tempo and rhythmic feel.

Example Entry:
```

Date: February 17, 2024
Tempo and Rhythmic Feel Exploration:
Tempo: 120 BPM
Rhythmic Feel: Swing
(Eighth notes with a swung feel)

Notation:
[Include a simple rhythmic notation or tablature]
Metronome Markings:
Quarter note = 120 BPM
```

Visual Representation:
[Include a visual representation of the swung feel]
Contextual Notes:
Exploring a slow swing feel for a melancholic ballad.
Experimenting with expressive phrasing and dynamics
within the context of the swung eighth notes.
```

By documenting specific tempos and rhythmic feels in your musical diary, you create a detailed reference that guides your playing and serves as a valuable resource for future performances or developments of your guitar compositions.

ARE THERE INFLUENCES FROM OTHER GENRES OR STYLES?

Explore whether your musical idea draws influences from other genres or styles. How do these influences contribute to the uniqueness of your composition?

Exploring influences from other genres or styles in your guitar composition can contribute to the uniqueness and richness of your musical ideas.

Here are some ways to identify and document these influences in your musical diary:

Identifying Influences

Listen Widely: Explore a diverse range of musical genres and styles to expose yourself to different techniques, rhythms, and tonalities.

Analyze Favorites: Consider your favorite artists, bands, or compositions. Identify elements that resonate with you, whether it's a specific chord progression, a rhythmic feel, or a melodic approach.

Cross-Genre Exploration: Don't limit yourself to one genre. Experiment with blending elements from various genres to create a unique fusion.

Example:
```

Influences:
Jazz for harmonic complexity
Folk for storytelling melodies
Electronic for atmospheric textures
```


Documenting Influences

Genre and Style List: Create a list of genres and styles that influence your composition. Be specific about elements from each genre that inspire you.

Reference Artists: Note specific artists or bands within each genre that have influenced your approach. This provides a reference point for your creative process.

Musical Traits: Document the musical traits or characteristics you draw from each influence. This could include harmonic progressions, rhythmic patterns, instrumentation, or tonal qualities.

Example:
```
Musical Diary Entry:
Genres and Styles:
Jazz
Folk
```

Electronic
Reference Artists:
John Coltrane (Jazz)
Nick Drake (Folk)
Tycho (Electronic)
Musical Traits:
Jazz: Exploring extended chords and modal interchange
Folk: Embracing storytelling through lyrics and melodies
Electronic: Incorporating ambient textures and electronic production techniques
```

## *Creative Integration*

**Blend Elements**: Experiment with integrating elements from different genres into your composition. This could involve incorporating a jazz chord progression into a folk-inspired melody or infusing electronic textures into a traditional structure.

**Unexpected Pairings**: Explore unexpected pairings of genres to create a fresh and innovative sound. The juxtaposition of contrasting elements can lead to unique and captivating compositions.

**Example**:
```

Creative Integration:
Jazz-inspired chord voicings in a folk-style ballad
Electronic beats and textures in a traditional blues progression
```
```

Genre Fusion Exploration

Genre Fusion Exercises: Dedicate specific sessions to experimenting with genre fusion. This could involve taking a melody from one genre and reimagining it with the rhythmic feel or instrumentation of another.

Mix and Match: Mix and match different aspects of genres to create a hybrid composition. For example, blend the storytelling approach of folk with the intricate rhythms of Afrobeat.

Example:
```

Genre Fusion Exploration:
Folk melody with a bossa nova rhythm
Blues progression with elements of Indian classical music
```

Reflection and Analysis

Reflect on Integration: After experimenting with genre influences, reflect on how well different elements integrate into your composition. Consider what enhances the overall mood and character.

Analyze Impact: Analyze the impact of these influences on your composition. How do they contribute to the uniqueness of your musical idea? Identify specific moments or sections where genre influences are prominently felt.

Example:

```

Reflection and Analysis:
The jazz-inspired chord voicings added a layer of sophistication to the folk ballad without overshadowing its intimate storytelling.
The electronic textures elevated the atmospheric quality of the composition, creating a sense of modernity within a traditional structure.
```


Contextual Notes

Contextual Notes: Write down any contextual notes about your influences, such as your mood, experiences, or external factors shaping your musical exploration.
Example:
```

Date: February 17, 2024
Contextual Notes:
Inspired by a recent jazz concert
Reflecting on the storytelling aspect of folk music
Exploring electronic production techniques after listening to ambient electronic artists
```

By documenting influences from other genres or styles in your musical diary, you create a comprehensive reference that not only honors your inspirations but also serves as a roadmap for the creative integration of diverse elements into your guitar compositions.

By asking yourself these questions, you'll create a comprehensive record of your musical ideas in your diary. This documentation not only serves as a reference for your composition process but also provides valuable insights into the creative choices and intentions behind your guitar compositions.

DOCUMENTING DREAMS AND ASPIRATIONS

Include your dreams, aspirations, and goals in your musical diary. Consider how these dreams can shape the direction and purpose of your composition. Musical themes can often arise from personal aspirations.

Recording your dreams and aspirations in your musical diary for guitar composition involves connecting personal aspirations to musical expression.

Here are some questions to help you articulate and document your dreams and aspirations in a way that can influence your guitar composition:

WHAT ARE MY LONG-TERM MUSICAL GOALS?

Reflect on your broader musical ambitions. Are there specific milestones or achievements you aspire to in your musical journey? Consider how these long-term goals can shape the direction of your composition.

Reflecting on your broader musical ambitions and considering long-term goals is a crucial aspect of shaping the direction of your guitar composition. Setting clear and meaningful long-term goals can provide a sense of purpose and guide your creative journey.

Let's think about how to reflect on your musical ambitions and set long-term goals:

Define Your Musical Ambitions

Reflect on Passion: Consider what aspects of music ignite your passion. Whether it's composing, performing, collaborating, or exploring different genres, understanding your musical passions is the first step.

Identify Influences: Think about musicians, bands, or composers who inspire you. Identify the elements of their musical journeys that resonate with your own ambitions.

Example:

```

Musical Ambitions:
Create emotionally resonant compositions
Develop a unique fingerstyle guitar technique
Collaborate with musicians from diverse genres
```

Consider Long-Term Vision

Envision Your Musical Future: Imagine where you see yourself as a musician in the long term. This could involve envisioning specific achievements, recognition, or the impact you want to have on your audience.

Example:

```

Long-Term Vision:
Performing original compositions in renowned music venues
Recording and releasing a full-length album
Establishing a musical project that merges various genres and cultural influences
```

Set Specific Milestones

Break Down Goals: Divide your long-term vision into specific, achievable milestones. These could be intermediate accomplishments that contribute to your broader ambitions.

Timeline: Assign a timeline to each milestone. This helps create a roadmap for your musical journey and provides a sense of progression.

Example:
```

Milestones:

Complete a set of 5 original compositions within the next 6 months

Perform at a local open mic night within the next 3 months

Collaborate with a percussionist on a fusion project within the next year
```

Balance Specific and Flexible Goals

Specific Goals: Set clear, specific goals that provide direction and focus. These could include technical achievements, compositional milestones, or performance goals.

Flexible Goals: Allow for flexibility in your goals to adapt to unexpected opportunities or shifts in your creative journey. This ensures you remain open to new possibilities.

Example:
```

Specific Goal:
```

Learn and master a challenging fingerstyle technique within the next 3 months
Flexible Goal:
Explore collaborations with musicians from different cultural backgrounds as opportunities arise
```

## Align with Personal Values

**Connect with Values**: Ensure that your long-term musical goals align with your personal values and principles. This connection adds depth and authenticity to your creative journey.
**Example**:
```

Personal Values:
Cultural diversity and inclusivity
Emotional expression through music
Continuous learning and growth
```

## Regularly Evaluate and Adjust

**Periodic Reflection**: Schedule regular times for reflection on your musical goals. Assess your progress, celebrate achievements, and identify areas for improvement.
**Adjust Goals**: Be open to adjusting your goals based on evolving interests, experiences, or unexpected opportunities. Goals should be dynamic and responsive to your changing creative landscape.
**Example**:
```

```

Periodic Reflection:
Monthly reflection on progress and adjustments to goals
Consideration of new musical genres or techniques that spark interest
```

Document in Your Musical Diary

Record Goals: Document your long-term musical goals in your musical diary. Include the specific milestones, timeline, and any contextual notes about your aspirations.

Reflective Entries: Use your diary to reflect on your progress, challenges, and moments of inspiration. This becomes a valuable record of your musical journey.

Example Entry:
```

*Date: February 17, 2024*
*Musical Goals:*
*Short-Term Goal:*
*Complete the composition of a new piece by the end of the month*
*Intermediate Goal:*
*Collaborate with a vocalist on a songwriting project within the next 6 months*
*Long-Term Vision:*
*Perform at a major music festival within the next 2 years*
*Reflective Notes:*
```

Explored new chord progressions and lyrical themes for the upcoming composition

Reached out to a local vocalist for potential collaboration

Researched opportunities to apply for upcoming music festivals

```
```

By reflecting on your broader musical ambitions and setting long-term goals, you create a roadmap that guides your creative journey and shapes the direction of your guitar compositions. Regularly revisiting and adjusting these goals ensures that your musical aspirations remain aligned with your evolving creative vision.

HOW CAN MUSIC REFLECT MY PERSONAL ASPIRATIONS?

Explore how music, specifically your guitar composition, can serve as a reflection of your personal aspirations. How can musical elements convey the essence of your goals and dreams?

Music, especially through guitar composition, has the remarkable ability to serve as a reflection of personal aspirations. The elements and nuances within a composition can convey the essence of one's goals and dreams.

Read on to learn how musical elements can correlate with personal aspirations and how to infuse your guitar composition with these reflections:

Identifying Personal Aspirations

Self-Reflection: Take time to reflect on your broader life goals, dreams, and personal aspirations. Consider what motivates and inspires you beyond the realm of music.

Artistic Expression: Think about how your artistic expression through guitar composition can align with or convey elements of your personal journey and aspirations.

Example:
```

Personal Aspirations:
Cultivate a sense of inner peace and tranquility
Convey stories of resilience and overcoming challenges
Foster connections and unity through shared musical experiences
```

Emotional Resonance Through Chord Progressions

Choose Expressive Chords: Select chord progressions that resonate emotionally with your personal aspirations. Minor chords for reflection, major chords for optimism, or extended chords for complexity can convey specific moods.

Example:
```

Chord Progression:
Minor chords for reflective moments
Major chords for uplifting and optimistic sections
```

Extended chords for harmonic richness and complexity
```

## Melodic Storytelling

**Craft Melodies with Purpose**: Shape melodies that tell a story or evoke emotions related to your personal aspirations. Consider the rise and fall of notes to convey the highs and lows of your journey.

**Example**:
```

Melodic Storytelling:
Soaring melodies for moments of triumph
Gentle, flowing lines for reflective and contemplative passages
Staccato motifs for moments of resilience and determination
```

## Dynamic Symbolism

**Dynamic Changes**: Use dynamic shifts in your composition to symbolize the ebb and flow of life. Gradual builds and sudden drops can mirror the dynamics of personal growth and challenges.

**Example**:
```

Dynamic Symbolism:
Gradual crescendos for personal growth and development

Sudden dynamic drops for moments of reflection or vulnerability
```

## Rhythmic Representations

**Symbolic Rhythms**: Experiment with rhythmic patterns that symbolize the rhythm of life. Syncopated rhythms for unpredictability, steady pulses for stability, or irregular patterns for uniqueness.

**Example**:
```

Rhythmic Representations:
Syncopated rhythms for moments of unpredictability
Steady, driving pulses for a sense of stability and determination
Irregular patterns to highlight the uniqueness of personal experiences
```

## Instrumentation Choices

**Personal Instrumentation**: Consider the choice of instruments and their symbolic significance. Each instrument can represent a facet of your personality, aspirations, or the diverse elements of your journey.

**Example**:
```

Instrumentation Choices:
Acoustic guitar for intimacy and introspection
String section for added emotional depth and richness

Percussion for rhythmic vitality and energy
```

## Lyricism and Narrative

**Conveying Stories**: If your composition includes lyrics, craft them with intentional storytelling. Use metaphor and imagery to convey elements of your personal aspirations and the narrative of your journey.

**Example**:
```

Lyricism and Narrative:
Metaphors of nature to symbolize personal growth
Stories of overcoming challenges and finding inner strength
Expressing a sense of unity and connection through shared experiences
``

Integrate Personal Experiences

Draw from Experiences: Infuse your composition with musical reflections on specific life experiences related to your aspirations. This authenticity enhances the connection between your personal journey and the music.
Example:
```

Integration of Personal Experiences:
Drawing inspiration from a challenging period and expressing resilience through the music
```

Crafting melodies inspired by moments of personal triumph

Reflecting on shared musical experiences and their impact on personal connections
```

## Long-Term Musical Goals

**Align with Aspirations**: Set long-term musical goals that align with your broader life aspirations. Whether it's recording an album, performing on a certain stage, or collaborating with specific artists, ensure these goals contribute to your overall life narrative.

**Example**:
```

Long-Term Musical Goals:
Record an album that reflects personal growth and resilience
Perform on a stage known for its intimate and reflective ambiance
Collaborate with artists who share a similar vision of using music to connect and inspire
```

## Documenting in Your Musical Diary

**Reflective Entries**: Write reflective entries in your musical diary, documenting how each musical element aligns with your personal aspirations.

**Goal Progress**: Track the progress of long-term musical goals in your diary. Celebrate milestones
```

and acknowledge the role each composition plays in shaping your journey.

Example Entry:
```

*Date: February 17, 2024*
*Reflective Entry:*
*Today's composition reflects my aspiration for inner peace. The gentle chord progressions and soaring melodies mirror the journey of finding tranquility amidst life's challenges. The rhythmic patterns symbolize the unpredictable yet beautiful rhythm of life. Excited to see how these elements evolve in future compositions as I continue to explore and express my personal aspirations through music.*
```

By intentionally infusing your guitar composition with elements that reflect your personal aspirations, you create a musical narrative that goes beyond mere notes and chords. This approach transforms your music into a powerful and authentic expression of your journey, allowing both you and your listeners to connect with the deeper meaning within the soundwaves.

WHAT EMOTIONS ARE ASSOCIATED WITH MY ASPIRATIONS?

Consider the emotions tied to your aspirations. Are they characterized by excitement, determination, hope, or a combination of feelings? How can you translate these emotions into musical expression?

Extracting emotions from personal aspirations and translating them into musical expression is a deeply personal and intuitive process. Music has the power to convey a wide range of emotions, and your guitar composition can serve as a canvas for expressing the depth of your feelings.

Here's how to extract emotions from personal aspirations and document them in your musical diary:

Identify Core Emotions

Reflect on Aspirations: Consider the core emotions associated with your personal aspirations. What feelings do you hope to evoke or convey through your music?
Example Emotions:
Joy
Longing
Resilience
Tranquility
Passion
Reflection

Connect Emotions to Specific Aspirations

Emotional Mapping: Associate each core emotion with a specific aspect of your personal aspirations. This creates a direct **link** between the emotional landscape and the narrative of your journey.
Example:
```

Emotional Mapping:
```

Joy: Celebrating moments of triumph and achievement

Longing: Expressing a yearning for growth and exploration

Resilience: Conveying strength and determination in overcoming challenges

Tranquility: Creating moments of calm and introspection

Passion: Infusing energy and enthusiasm into the composition

Reflection: Capturing introspective and contemplative moods
```

## *Translate Emotions into Musical Elements*

**Melodic Choices**: Choose melodic motifs that reflect the emotional nuances. Ascending lines for joy, descending phrases for reflection, or repeated patterns for resilience.

**Example:**
```

Melodic Choices:
Joy: Upward arpeggios and bright major scales
Reflection: Descending phrases and contemplative melodies
Resilience: Repeated motifs and strong, assertive melodies
```

## *Harmonic Palette*
```

Harmonic Progressions: Experiment with harmonies that mirror the emotional landscape. Majestic chords for joy, open chords for tranquility, or dissonant chords for moments of tension.

Example:
```

Harmonic Palette:
Joy: Major seventh and augmented chords for a triumphant feel
Tranquility: Open chords and suspended harmonies for a serene atmosphere
Tension: Dissonant intervals and unresolved chords for moments of challenge
```

Rhythmic Expressiveness

Rhythmic Patterns: Use rhythmic variations to convey emotion. Syncopated rhythms for excitement, slow tempos for reflection, or dynamic changes for expressive impact.

Example:
```

Rhythmic Expressiveness:
Excitement: Upbeat, syncopated rhythms and fast tempos
Reflection: Slow, deliberate tempos with spacious pauses
Expressive Impact: Dynamic changes and rhythmic accents for emphasis
```

Dynamic Shaping

Dynamic Contrasts: Utilize dynamic changes to shape the emotional arc of your composition. Gradual builds for intensity, sudden drops for vulnerability, and nuanced dynamics for subtlety.

Example:
```

Dynamic Shaping:
Intensity: Gradual crescendos and dynamic swells
Vulnerability: Sudden dynamic drops and quiet passages
Subtlety: Nuanced dynamics with delicate phrasing
```

Instrumentation Choices

Instrumental Colors: Choose instruments that enhance the emotional palette. Warm tones for tranquility, bright timbres for joy, or a blend of contrasting instruments for complexity.

Example:
```

Instrumentation Choices:
Tranquility: Acoustic guitar with subtle strings and gentle percussion
Joy: Electric guitar with a vibrant brass section and rhythmic drums
Complexity: Layered instrumentation with a mix of acoustic and electronic elements
```

Expressive Techniques

Extended Techniques: Explore expressive techniques to convey specific emotions. Vibrato for warmth, slides for yearning, or tapping for excitement.

Example:
```

Expressive Techniques:
Warmth: Gentle vibrato and legato phrasing
Yearning: Slides and bending for expressive melodic contours
Excitement: Percussive tapping and dynamic fingerstyle techniques
```

Tempo and Pacing

Tempo Choices: Select tempos that align with the emotional intensity. Upbeat tempos for lively moments, slow tempos for contemplation, or tempo changes to convey shifts in mood.

Example:
```

Tempo and Pacing:
Lively Moments: Fast tempos with energetic rhythms
Contemplation: Slow tempos with spacious phrasing
Shifts in Mood: Tempo changes to reflect emotional transitions
```

Documenting in Your Musical Diary

Emotional Annotations: Write down emotional annotations in your musical diary for each section of your composition. Describe the feelings you aim to convey and how specific musical elements achieve this.

Example Entry:
```

*Date: February 17, 2024*
*Emotional Annotations:*
*Joyful Section:*
*Upbeat tempo, major seventh chords, vibrant instrumentation*
*Aim to convey a sense of triumph and celebration*
*Reflective Interlude:*
*Slow tempo, delicate fingerpicking, suspended harmonies*
*Create a moment of introspection and contemplation*
*Resilient Climax:*
*Dynamic builds, rhythmic intensity, assertive melodies*
*Express strength and determination in overcoming challenges*
```

By consciously connecting your personal aspirations with specific emotions and translating them into musical elements, you infuse your guitar composition with a profound sense of authenticity.

This intentional approach allows your music to become a powerful conduit for expressing the intricate tapestry of your emotional landscape and personal journey.

ARE THERE SPECIFIC THEMES OR CONCEPTS

RELATED TO MY DREAMS?

Identify any overarching themes or concepts related to your dreams and aspirations. How can these themes be translated into musical motifs, chord progressions, or overall composition structures?

Identifying overarching themes or concepts related to your dreams and aspirations can provide a strong foundation for translating these ideas into musical motifs, chord progressions, and overall guitar composition structures.

Let's learn about some ways to extract themes from dreams and aspirations and weave them into your musical diary for guitar composition:

Reflection on Dreams and Aspirations

Self-Reflection: Take time to introspect and identify recurring themes or overarching concepts related to your dreams and aspirations. Consider the emotions, imagery, or narratives that consistently emerge.

Example Themes/Concepts:
Journeys and Exploration
Inner Growth and Resilience
Connection and Unity
Nature and Tranquility
Personal Triumphs and Challenges
Transformation and Metamorphosis
Translating Themes into Musical Elements:
Motif Creation: Create musical motifs that directly represent the identified themes or concepts. These

motifs can serve as musical building blocks that recur throughout your composition.

Example:
```

Theme: Journeys and Exploration
Motif:
Upward arpeggios representing ascent and progress
Descending phrases for moments of reflection and descent
Shifting key signatures to evoke the sense of exploration
```

Chord Progressions and Harmonic Choices

Harmonic Symbolism: Choose chord progressions that symbolize the identified themes. Majestic chords for triumph, open harmonies for connection, or modal interchange for transformation.

Example:
```

Theme: Inner Growth and Resilience
Chord Progression:
Embracing minor chords for resilience
Gradual progression to major chords for growth
Suspended chords for moments of anticipation and reflection
```

Structural Considerations

Sectional Organization: Organize your composition into distinct sections, each representing a different facet of your overarching themes. This could include an introductory section, a developmental middle section, and a climactic resolution.

Example:
```

Theme: Nature and Tranquility
Structural Considerations:
Introductory Section: Gentle fingerpicking and open chords to set a tranquil tone
Developmental Middle Section: Increasing complexity in instrumentation, mimicking the dynamic nature of natural environments
Climactic Resolution: Returning to a serene state with a resolution in the final section
```

Instrumentation Choices

Instrumental Palette: Select instruments that complement the chosen themes. Acoustic guitars for introspection, strings for emotional depth, or percussion for rhythmic vitality.

Example:
```

Theme: Connection and Unity
Instrumentation Choices:
Acoustic guitars for intimate connection
String section for added emotional depth
Percussion for rhythmic unity and vitality
```

Expressive Techniques

Techniques to Enhance Themes: Use expressive techniques that enhance the emotional impact of your chosen themes. Techniques such as harmonics, slides, or vibrato can add depth and nuance.

Example:
```

Theme: Personal Triumphs and Challenges
Expressive Techniques:
Vibrato for expressing triumph
Dynamic slides to represent overcoming challenges
Percussive techniques for moments of impact and resilience
```

Melodic Storytelling

Narrative through Melodies: Craft melodies that tell a story related to the overarching themes. Consider the rise and fall of notes, melodic contour, and motifs that convey specific emotions.

Example:
```

Theme: Transformation and Metamorphosis
Melodic Storytelling:
Shifting melodies to represent transformation
Repetitive motifs for the cyclical nature of metamorphosis
Gradual crescendos and decrescendos to mimic the ebb and flow of change
```

```

## **Documenting in Your Musical Diary**

**Theme Annotations**: Write down theme annotations in your musical diary for each section of your composition. Describe the feelings and concepts associated with each theme and how they manifest in the music.

**Example Entry**:
```

Date: February 17, 2024
Theme Annotations:
Journeys and Exploration:
Upward arpeggios and shifting key signatures to convey progress and exploration
Inner Growth and Resilience:
Chord progressions transitioning from minor to major for resilience and growth
Nature and Tranquility:
Structural considerations, such as an introductory section with gentle fingerpicking, representing the serene quality of nature
Connection and Unity:
Instrumentation choices, including acoustic guitars, strings, and percussion for a sense of unity and connection
Personal Triumphs and Challenges:
Expressive techniques like vibrato and percussive techniques for moments of triumph and resilience
Transformation and Metamorphosis:
Melodic storytelling through shifting melodies and repetitive motifs to represent the transformative journey

```

By extracting overarching themes or concepts from your dreams and aspirations and translating them into musical elements, you create a composition that goes beyond notes and chords. Your guitar composition becomes a deeply evocative expression of your personal narrative and the profound themes that shape your journey.

## WHAT GENRE OR STYLE ALIGNS WITH MY ASPIRATIONS?

Explore the musical genres or styles that resonate with your aspirations. Are there specific genres that capture the spirit of your dreams? Consider incorporating elements from these genres into your composition.

Aligning specific musical genres with aspirations and dreams can be a creative and inspiring approach to document in your musical diary for guitar composition. Different genres evoke distinct emotions and moods, making them suitable for expressing various themes.

### *Folk for Storytelling and Connection*

**Aspiration**: Connection and Unity
**Dream Theme**: Creating a sense of community through shared experiences
**Example Musical Diary Entry:**
```

Genre: Folk
Aspiration Theme: Connection and Unity

Dream Theme: Fostering community through shared stories

Musical Approach:

Acoustic fingerpicking for an intimate connection

Reflective lyrics to convey personal narratives

Simple chord progressions to emphasize universal themes

Today's composition in the folk genre aims to capture the essence of connection and unity. The acoustic fingerpicking and storytelling lyrics weave a narrative of shared experiences, creating an intimate connection with the listener. The simplicity of the chord progressions serves to emphasize universal themes, fostering a sense of community through the power of music.

```

Jazz for Exploration and Innovation

Aspiration: Journeys and Exploration

Dream Theme: Embarking on a musical journey filled with innovation and creativity

Example Musical Diary Entry:

```

*Genre: Jazz*

*Aspiration Theme: Journeys and Exploration*

*Dream Theme: Embarking on a musical journey filled with innovation and creativity*

*Musical Approach:*

*Complex chord progressions and modal interchange for musical exploration*

*Improvisational elements to capture the spirit of a musical journey*
```

Syncopated rhythms and dynamic changes for added excitement

Today's jazz-inspired composition embodies the theme of journeys and exploration. The intricate chord progressions and modal interchange create a sense of musical exploration, while improvisational elements capture the spontaneous spirit of a journey. Syncopated rhythms and dynamic changes add excitement and energy to the overall composition, symbolizing the thrill of pushing creative boundaries.

```
```

Ambient for Tranquility and Reflection

Aspiration: Inner Peace and Tranquility
Dream Theme: Creating a sonic landscape that fosters introspection and calm
Example Musical Diary Entry:

```
```

Genre: Ambient
Aspiration Theme: Inner Peace and Tranquility
Dream Theme: Creating a sonic landscape that fosters introspection and calm
Musical Approach:
Ethereal and atmospheric textures to evoke a sense of calm
Slow tempos and sustained chords for introspective moments
Minimalistic instrumentation to create a tranquil sonic space
Today's ambient composition is dedicated to the aspiration of inner peace and tranquility. The ethereal and

atmospheric textures aim to create a sonic landscape that fosters introspection and calm. Slow tempos and sustained chords contribute to moments of reflection, while the minimalistic instrumentation enhances the overall sense of a tranquil sonic space.

```

### Blues for Resilience and Triumph

**Aspiration**: Personal Triumphs and Challenges
**Dream Theme**: Expressing resilience and triumph through the blues
**Example Musical Diary Entry**:
```

Genre: Blues
Aspiration Theme: Personal Triumphs and Challenges
Dream Theme: Expressing resilience and triumph through the blues
Musical Approach:
Soulful guitar solos to convey emotional depth
Minor pentatonic scales for moments of challenge
Upbeat and assertive rhythms to signify triumph
Example Entry: Today's blues-inspired composition channels the theme of personal triumphs and challenges. The soulful guitar solos convey emotional depth, while the use of minor pentatonic scales captures moments of challenge and reflection. The upbeat and assertive rhythms symbolize the triumph over adversity, creating a musical narrative that speaks to resilience and strength.
```
```

Electronic for Transformation and Metamorphosis

Aspiration: Transformation and Metamorphosis
Dream Theme: Crafting a sonic journey of metamorphosis through electronic elements
Example Musical Diary Entry:
```

*Genre: Electronic*
*Aspiration Theme: Transformation and Metamorphosis*
*Dream Theme: Crafting a sonic journey of metamorphosis through electronic elements*
*Musical Approach:*
*Ambient synthesizers and electronic textures for a transformative atmosphere*
*Dynamic and evolving soundscapes to represent metamorphosis*
*Experimental production techniques for creative innovation*
*Today's electronic composition is dedicated to the theme of transformation and metamorphosis. The ambient synthesizers and electronic textures create a transformative atmosphere, while dynamic and evolving soundscapes represent the journey of metamorphosis. Experimental production techniques add a layer of creative innovation, crafting a sonic narrative that mirrors the theme of transformation.*
```

Classical for Elegance and Grace

Aspiration: Elegance and Grace

Dream Theme: Conveying a sense of sophistication and refined beauty through classical composition

Example Musical Diary Entry:
```

*Genre: Classical*

*Aspiration Theme: Elegance and Grace*

*Dream Theme: Conveying a sense of sophistication and refined beauty through classical composition*

*Musical Approach:*

*Ornate and intricate melodies for a sense of elegance*

*Symphonic arrangements to enhance refined beauty*

*Formal structure and attention to detail for a classical touch*

*Today's classical composition is dedicated to the theme of elegance and grace. The ornate and intricate melodies aim to convey a sense of elegance, while symphonic arrangements enhance the overall refined beauty. The formal structure and meticulous attention to detail contribute to the classical touch, creating a musical piece that embodies sophistication.*
```

By aligning specific musical genres with your aspirations and dreams, you can create compositions that not only resonate with your personal journey but also showcase the versatility of musical expression. Each genre becomes a unique palette for translating diverse themes into evocative and meaningful guitar compositions.

DO MY ASPIRATIONS HAVE A NARRATIVE OR STORY?

Consider whether your aspirations can be framed within a narrative or story. How can your guitar composition tell a musical story that mirrors the journey toward your aspirations?

In the context of guitar composition, a narrative arc refers to the overarching structure and progression of a musical piece that tells a story or conveys a specific emotional journey. It involves guiding the listener through various stages, each with its own unique characteristics, building a cohesive and engaging musical experience. Creating a narrative arc for your guitar composition involves careful consideration of elements like dynamics, tempo, harmony, melody, and instrumentation to convey a clear and compelling narrative.

Framing your dreams and aspirations into a narrative through your guitar composition involves creating a musical story that mirrors the journey toward your goals. This process allows you to convey the emotional and thematic elements of your aspirations, translating them into a cohesive and evocative musical experience.

Here are some ways to frame your dreams into a narrative through your guitar composition:

Identify Key Themes and Emotions

Reflection: Begin by identifying the key themes and emotions associated with your dreams and aspirations. Consider the overarching narrative you want to convey through your music.

Example:
Dream Theme: Personal Growth and Exploration
Emotional Elements: Joy, Resilience, Contemplation

Create a Structural Outline

Storyboarding: Map out a structural outline for your composition, dividing it into distinct sections that represent different phases of your journey. This can include an introduction, development, climax, and resolution.

Example:
Introduction: Establishing the initial state, perhaps with soft and reflective chords.

Development: Building up the narrative with dynamic shifts, representing challenges and growth.

Climax: A powerful section symbolizing the peak of your journey and triumphs.

Resolution: Concluding with a sense of resolution and reflection.

Use Melodic Motifs for Storytelling

Motif Development: Create melodic motifs that serve as musical characters in your story. These motifs can evolve and reappear, symbolizing the progression of your narrative.

Example:
Motif 1: Gentle and ascending motif for the introduction, representing the beginning of your journey.

Motif 2: A more complex and dynamic motif during the climax, signifying challenges and growth.

Motif 3: Resolving and reflective motif for the resolution, symbolizing the end of your journey.

Employ Dynamics and Tempo Changes

Dynamic Expression: Use dynamic changes to convey the emotional intensity of different story elements. Gradual builds and sudden drops can add a dynamic arc to your composition.

Example:

Soft Dynamics: Reflective and introspective moments.

Loud Dynamics: Triumphs and overcoming challenges.

Gradual Crescendos: Building anticipation and growth.

Experiment with Harmonic Progressions

Harmonic Palette: Choose harmonic progressions that align with the emotional tone of each section. Experiment with major and minor chords to convey contrasting moods.

Example:

Major Chords: Expressing joy and triumph.

Minor Chords: Reflecting challenges and contemplation.

Suspended Chords: Adding tension and anticipation.

Utilize Symbolic Instrumentation

Instrumental Choices: Select specific instruments that carry symbolic meaning. Different timbres can evoke distinct emotions and enhance the storytelling.

Example:

Acoustic Guitar: Personal and introspective moments.

Electric Guitar: Dynamic and triumphant sections.

Strings: Adding richness and depth to key moments.

Craft a Narrative Arc

Narrative Flow: Ensure that your composition follows a coherent narrative arc, guiding the listener through the ups and downs of your musical journey.

Example:

Introduction: Soft acoustic guitar with a gentle motif, setting the stage for the journey.

Development: Gradual buildup with dynamic shifts and intricate melodies, representing challenges and growth.

Climax: Powerful electric guitar solo and full instrumentation, symbolizing triumph and achievement.

Resolution: Subdued acoustic outro, concluding the narrative with a reflective motif.

Documenting in Your Musical Diary

Narrative Annotations: In your musical diary, document the narrative elements associated with each section. Describe the emotions, challenges, and triumphs expressed through the music.

Example Entry:
```

*Date: February 17, 2024*
*Narrative Annotations:*
*Introduction:*
*Soft acoustic guitar and gentle ascending motif, representing the beginning of the journey.*
*Development:*
*Gradual buildup with dynamic shifts and intricate melodies, symbolizing challenges and growth.*
*Climax:*
*Powerful electric guitar solo and full instrumentation, expressing triumph and achievement.*
*Resolution:*
*Subdued acoustic outro with a reflective motif, concluding the narrative with a sense of resolution.*
```

By framing your dreams and aspirations into a narrative through your guitar composition, you transform your musical journey into a compelling and immersive story. The intentional use of melodic motifs, dynamics, tempo changes, and symbolic instrumentation allows your composition to resonate not just as music but as a deeply personal and expressive narrative of your aspirations.

Let's go into a deeper dive on writing the important narrative arc for your guitar composition:

Introduction (Exposition)

Purpose: Set the stage for your musical narrative. Introduce key motifs, themes, or melodic elements that will be developed throughout the composition.

Musical Elements:

Soft dynamics

Gentle and reflective chords

Introduce a primary melodic motif

Example:
```

Introduction:
Soft acoustic guitar playing a simple and introspective motif
Reflective chords with minimal harmonic movement
Establishing a melodic theme that will evolve throughout the piece
```

Development (Rising Action)

Purpose: Build tension, complexity, and emotion. Develop the initial motifs, introducing variations and exploring different harmonic, rhythmic, and melodic elements.

Musical Elements:

Gradual increase in dynamics

Intricate melodies and chord progressions

Rising shtensity to create anticipation

Example:
```

Development:
Gradual increase in dynamics, adding layers to the instrumentation
```

Intricate guitar solos exploring different melodic variations

Rising intensity through dynamic shifts and expanded harmonies
```

## Climax (Climactic Moment)

**Purpose**: Reach the emotional peak of the narrative. This section is often the most intense and expressive, representing the climax of your musical story.

**Musical Elements**:

Loud dynamics

Powerful guitar solos or intense instrumental sections

Complex harmonies and dynamic rhythmic patterns

**Example**:
```

Climax:

Loud and dynamic guitar solo expressing heightened emotion

Intense instrumental sections with full instrumentation

Complex harmonies and dynamic rhythmic patterns for maximum impact
```

## Falling Action (Release of Tension)

**Purpose**: Ease the tension built during the climax. Transition to a more subdued and reflective state, allowing for resolution and reflection.
```

Musical Elements:

Gradual decrease in dynamics

Simplified melodic motifs or variations

Transition to more open and resolved harmonies

Example:
```

Falling Action:

Gradual decrease in dynamics, releasing the built tension

Simplified melodic motifs or variations of themes introduced earlier

Transition to more open and resolved harmonies, preparing for resolution
```

Resolution (Conclusion)

Purpose: Provide closure to the narrative. Bring the composition to a satisfying and conclusive end, often revisiting and resolving the initial motifs.

Musical Elements:

Soft dynamics

Conclusive and resolved chord progressions

Revisiting and concluding the primary melodic motifs

Example:
```

Resolution:

Soft and gentle dynamics for a calming effect

Conclusive and resolved chord progressions providing a sense of closure
```

Revisiting and concluding the primary melodic motifs introduced in the introduction
```

## *Documenting in Your Musical Diary*

**Narrative Annotations**: In your musical diary, document the narrative arc by describing the emotional and thematic elements associated with each section. Include details on dynamics, harmonies, melodies, and the overall progression of the composition.

**Example Entry**:
```

Date: February 17, 2024
Narrative Arc Annotations:
Introduction:
Soft and reflective acoustic guitar introducing a melodic motif.
Development:
Gradual increase in dynamics with intricate guitar solos and rising intensity.
Climax:
Loud and dynamic guitar solo expressing heightened emotion with intense instrumental sections.
Falling Action:
Gradual decrease in dynamics, releasing tension with simplified melodic motifs.
Resolution:
Soft and gentle dynamics, providing closure with conclusive and resolved chord progressions.
```
```

By crafting a narrative arc in your guitar composition, you guide your listeners through a meaningful and emotional journey. The intentional use of musical elements at each stage enhances the storytelling aspect of your composition, creating a cohesive and engaging narrative that mirrors the progression of your aspirations and dreams.

CAN I CREATE MUSICAL SYMBOLS OR MOTIFS REPRESENTING MY DREAMS?

Explore the possibility of creating musical symbols or motifs that symbolize your dreams and aspirations. These could be recurring themes or musical gestures that carry specific meaning.

Musical Symbols and Their Meanings

Musical symbols are graphical notations used in sheet music to convey specific instructions to musicians regarding the performance of a piece. These symbols provide information about pitch, rhythm, dynamics, articulation, and other musical elements. While some symbols are standard and widely recognized, others may be specific to a particular composition or style.

Common Musical Symbols

Treble Clef: Indicates the pitch range for higher notes.

Bass Clef: Specifies the pitch range for lower notes.

Time Signature: Denotes the number of beats in a measure and the type of note that receives one beat.

Key Signature: Indicates the key of the composition and the arrangement of sharps or flats.

Tempo Markings: Indicate the speed at which the piece should be played (e.g., allegro, adagio).

Dynamics: Express the volume level, ranging from pianissimo (very soft) to fortissimo (very loud).

Articulations: Include symbols for legato (smooth), staccato (short and detached), and more.

Rests: Signify periods of silence, allowing the musician to refrain from playing.

Repeat Signs: Instruct the musician to go back and play a section of music again.

Creating Musical Symbols for Dreams and Aspirations

Creating musical symbols that symbolize dreams and aspirations involves incorporating visual elements that evoke a sense of inspiration, growth, and personal journey.

Ascendant Arrows: Use upward-pointing arrows to symbolize growth, progress, and the ascent towards dreams and aspirations. This can be incorporated into notations to suggest rising pitch or increasing dynamics.

Spirals: Representing a journey or transformation, spirals can be used to indicate a melodic motif that evolves throughout the composition, reflecting the twists and turns of one's aspirations.

Open Doorways: Symbolize opportunities and possibilities by incorporating open doorways into the musical score. This can be placed at key points in the composition to mark significant moments.

Tree Branches: Depicting growth and branching out, tree branches can be used as symbols for expanding melodic lines or harmonic progressions, representing the flourishing of dreams.

Mountains: Representing challenges and achievements, mountain symbols can be integrated into the score to mark climactic moments in the composition, symbolizing overcoming obstacles.

Crescent Moons: Indicating reflection and contemplation, crescent moons can be used to suggest softer dynamics or quieter passages in the composition, emphasizing introspective moments.

Feathers: Conveying a sense of lightness and freedom, feathers can be incorporated into the notation to symbolize moments of musical delicacy or grace within the composition.

Hourglass: Signifying the passage of time and the temporality of dreams, an hourglass symbol can be used to guide musicians through tempo changes or rhythmic variations.

Using Symbols in a Composition

When integrating these symbols into your guitar composition, consider their placement and repetition to create a coherent visual language. For example, using ascending arrows in conjunction with a melodic motif that gradually rises can reinforce the theme of growth and progress.

Additionally, you can annotate your musical diary with explanations of these symbols, providing insight into their intended meanings. This visual storytelling adds an extra layer of depth to your composition, allowing performers and listeners to connect with the narrative behind the music.

ARE THERE INSPIRATIONAL FIGURES OR INFLUENCES I CAN DRAW FROM?

Identify inspirational figures or influences related to your aspirations. How have musicians or artists who achieved similar dreams inspired you? Can you infuse elements of their style into your composition?

Here are some influential figures whose stories and work may serve as inspiration for your guitar composition, providing rich material to write about in your musical diary:

Johann Sebastian Bach (1685–1750)

Influence: A master of Baroque composition, Bach's intricate counterpoint, and expressive harmonies are timeless. His ability to convey deep emotions through music and his dedication to craftsmanship make him an enduring source of inspiration.

Wolfgang Amadeus Mozart (1756–1791)

Influence: A prodigy and prolific composer, Mozart's melodic brilliance and innovative use of form have left an indelible mark on classical music. His ability to convey both joy and profound emotion within his compositions can inspire a range of musical expressions.

Jimi Hendrix (1942–1970)

Influence: A pioneering figure in rock and blues, Hendrix's innovative guitar techniques and experimental approach to sound revolutionized the instrument's possibilities. His expressive playing and bold creativity continue to inspire guitarists across genres.

Andrés Segovia (1893–1987)

Influence: Revered as the father of the modern classical guitar movement, Segovia elevated the guitar to a concert instrument. His meticulous technique and commitment to expanding the guitar's repertoire make him an influential figure for aspiring classical guitarists.

B.B. King (1925–2015)

Influence: Known as the "King of the Blues," B.B. King's expressive and emotive guitar playing, along with his distinctive vibrato, has influenced generations of blues and rock musicians. His ability to convey profound feelings through the guitar is a testament to the instrument's emotive power.

Pat Metheny (b. 1954)

Influence: A versatile and innovative jazz guitarist, Metheny's work spans various styles, from traditional jazz to contemporary and fusion. His melodic phrasing and use of technology in guitar playing offer inspiration for those exploring diverse musical landscapes.

Django Reinhardt (1910–1953)

Influence: A pioneering figure in the world of jazz, Reinhardt's virtuosic gypsy jazz guitar playing and inventive improvisations continue to influence musicians today. His ability to blend traditional elements with innovation makes him a compelling source of inspiration.

Eddie Van Halen (1955–2020)

Influence: A groundbreaking guitarist in the rock genre, Eddie Van Halen's innovative use of the guitar's technical possibilities, including tapping and harmonics, has had a profound impact on rock and metal. His fearless approach to experimentation can inspire those seeking to push boundaries.

Paco de Lucía (1947–2014)

Influence: A flamenco guitar virtuoso, Paco de Lucía's unparalleled technique and emotional depth in playing have established him as one of the greatest guitarists in the flamenco tradition. His ability to convey intense emotions through the guitar can serve as a profound influence.

Nina Simone (1933–2003)

Influence: A renowned singer, songwriter, and pianist, Nina Simone's powerful voice and unique blend of jazz, blues, and soul convey a deep sense of emotion and social consciousness. Her ability to use music as a means of expression and activism is a testament to the transformative power of art.

When exploring these inspirational figures, consider delving into their life stories, musical journeys, and the specific elements of their compositions that resonate with your own aspirations. Writing about how their work influences and informs your musical diary can provide valuable insights into your own creative process and artistic development.

DO MY ASPIRATIONS INVOLVE COLLABORATIONS OR COMMUNITY?

Consider whether your aspirations involve collaboration or community engagement. How can your guitar composition reflect the idea of collaboration, unity, or shared experiences with others?

Infusing your guitar composition with the themes of collaboration, unity, or shared experiences involves incorporating musical elements that evoke a sense of togetherness and interconnectedness.

Here are some ways to achieve this in your guitar composition:

Harmonizing Melodies

Idea: Create harmonized melodies or counterpoint to symbolize collaboration and unity. This can involve multiple guitar parts playing complementary lines that blend together.

Example: In a section of your composition, have two guitar voices playing harmonized melodies, creating a rich and intertwined musical texture. This can be particularly effective in conveying a sense of collaboration and shared musical experiences.

Call and Response

Idea: Utilize call and response patterns between different sections or instruments. This musical dialogue represents communication and collaboration between musical elements.

Example: Have one guitar voice introduce a motif or phrase, and then have another guitar respond with a complementary or contrasting line. This back-and-forth creates a sense of musical conversation, reflecting shared experiences.

Ensemble Arrangement

Idea: Arrange your composition for a guitar ensemble, featuring multiple guitars playing different parts. Each guitar contributes to the overall musical tapestry, symbolizing unity and collaboration.

Example: Write parts for lead guitar, rhythm guitar, and perhaps additional guitars playing supporting roles. The combined sound of these elements working together reinforces the theme of collaboration and shared musical expression.

Chord Progressions with Shared Notes

Idea: Construct chord progressions where different chords share common tones, creating a harmonic connection between them. This can represent unity within the harmonic structure.

Example: Build a chord progression where each chord has at least one shared note with the preceding or succeeding chord. This shared tonality reinforces the sense of continuity and collaboration in the musical journey.

Dynamic Swells and Fades

Idea: Use dynamic swells and fades to signify collective rises and falls within the composition. This can symbolize a shared emotional journey or experience.

Example: Gradually increase the volume and intensity of the composition, reaching a peak, and then allow the dynamics to fade away collectively. This dynamic contour mirrors the ebb and flow of shared experiences.

Incorporate Percussion or Rhythm Elements

Idea: Introduce percussion or rhythm elements to create a sense of rhythmic unity. This can include fingerstyle techniques, percussive strumming, or even collaborative drumming patterns.

Example: Experiment with rhythmic patterns that involve multiple guitar techniques, such as tapping, slapping, or muted strums. The synchronized rhythm fosters a feeling of shared musical energy.

Modal Interchange

Idea: Use modal interchange to introduce unexpected chords or tonalities. This can represent the diversity within collaboration, showcasing different musical elements coming together.

Example: Incorporate chords from parallel or related keys, introducing harmonic shifts that add depth and complexity to the composition. The seamless integration of these diverse elements reflects collaborative exploration.

Coda or Finale

Idea: Conclude the composition with a collaborative finale or coda where all musical elements come together for a powerful and unified resolution.

Example: Build towards a final section where all guitars converge on a shared musical idea, creating a climactic and resonant conclusion that symbolizes the collective impact of the composition.

Remember that the key is to approach your composition with the intention of expressing collaboration, unity, or shared experiences. Experiment with different musical devices to find the combination that best resonates with the thematic elements you wish to convey in your guitar composition.

WHAT WOULD SUCCESS SOUND LIKE IN MUSICAL

TERMS?

Envision what success would sound like in musical terms. If you were to achieve your aspirations, how would that be expressed through the language of music? Consider the sonic qualities associated with success.

Envisioning success in musical terms for a guitar composition involves translating the emotional and psychological aspects of success into sonic qualities. Success is often associated with feelings of achievement, triumph, and fulfillment.

Here are ways to envision success and the sonic qualities that might accompany it in a guitar composition:

Dynamic Buildup

Sonic Quality: Gradual increase in dynamics to create a sense of rising energy and momentum.

Example: Start with soft and subtle guitar passages, then progressively build up to louder and more dynamic sections, mirroring the ascent towards success.

Upward Melodic Movement

Sonic Quality: Ascending melodic lines to symbolize progress, growth, and upward mobility.

Example: Incorporate melodies that move upward on the guitar neck, creating a sense of positivity and achievement. Utilize scales or arpeggios that naturally ascend.

Major Chord Resonance

Sonic Quality: Bright and resonant major chords associated with a positive and triumphant sound.

Example: Use major chords or open chord voicings to evoke a sense of optimism and accomplishment. Progressions that resolve to major chords can contribute to the overall feeling of success.

Energetic Rhythmic Patterns

Sonic Quality: Lively and energetic rhythmic patterns to convey a sense of vitality and enthusiasm.

Example: Experiment with upbeat strumming or picking patterns that drive the composition forward. Syncopated rhythms or percussive techniques can enhance the sense of energy.

Harmonic Richness

Sonic Quality: Rich harmonies and chord voicings to create a full and expansive sound.

Example: Explore extended chords, inversions, and harmonically dense progressions to add depth and complexity. The richness of the harmonies can evoke a sense of accomplishment and fullness.

Triumphant Crescendos

Sonic Quality: Crescendos leading to powerful climaxes, emphasizing the victorious nature of success.

Example: Build sections of your composition with a gradual increase in intensity, culminating in a triumphant climax. This can be achieved through rising dynamics, increased instrumentation, or both.

Expressive Guitar Techniques

Sonic Quality: Utilize expressive guitar techniques to convey emotion and intensity.

Example: Incorporate techniques like slides, bends, vibrato, and hammer-ons/pull-offs to add nuance and emotion to your playing. These techniques can help articulate the emotional depth associated with success.

Expansive Soundscapes

Sonic Quality: Create expansive and open soundscapes to represent the broad horizons and possibilities that come with success.

Example: Experiment with ambient effects, such as reverb and delay, to create a sense of space and openness. Long sustained notes and chords can contribute to the feeling of expansiveness.

Resolution in Concluding Sections

Sonic Quality: Resolve the composition with a sense of completeness and finality.

Example: Conclude your composition with chords or motifs that provide a satisfying resolution. This can create a sonic representation of reaching a successful endpoint.

Collaborative and Harmonious Elements

Sonic Quality: Collaborative musical elements working harmoniously to represent unity in success.

Example: If composing for multiple guitars, ensure that the different parts collaborate seamlessly, creating a unified sound. Harmonic progressions and melodies that complement each other contribute to a sense of harmony and success.

Envisioning success in musical terms for a guitar composition involves capturing the emotional essence of achievement and accomplishment. Experiment with these sonic qualities to create a composition that not only reflects the theme of success but also resonates with the listener on an emotional level.

HOW CAN I CAPTURE THE JOURNEY TOWARD MY ASPIRATIONS MUSICALLY?

Think about the journey toward your aspirations. Can your guitar composition capture the various stages of this journey, from initial inspiration to overcoming challenges and reaching milestones?

Capturing the various stages of a journey through guitar composition involves translating the emotions, challenges, and triumphs into musical expressions. Each stage can be represented by specific musical elements, creating a dynamic and narrative-driven composition.

Here are examples of how guitar composition can embody the different stages of a journey:

Initial Inspiration

Musical Elements: Uplifting Melodies: Create bright and uplifting melodic lines that capture the initial spark of inspiration.

Open Chord Progressions: Utilize open and expansive chord progressions to convey a sense of possibility and exploration.

Example: Begin the composition with a clean and arpeggiated guitar passage featuring major chords and a hopeful melody. This section represents the birth of a creative idea and the excitement of embarking on a journey.

Navigating Challenges

Musical Elements: Tension in Chord Progressions: Introduce dissonant or tense chord progressions to symbolize obstacles and challenges.

Dynamic Contrasts: Use sudden changes in dynamics to represent the highs and lows of facing difficulties.

Example: Transition to a section with darker, minor chords and dynamic contrasts, expressing the challenges encountered along the journey. Incorporate techniques like palm muting or percussive strumming to add a sense of tension.

Overcoming Obstacles

Musical Elements: Climactic Buildups: Gradual buildups leading to powerful musical peaks to symbolize overcoming obstacles.

Resolution in Chord Progressions: Shift to resolving chord progressions to signify triumph and resolution.

Example: Build the composition towards a climactic section featuring a soaring guitar solo or intense strumming patterns. Resolve the tension with a triumphant chord progression, symbolizing the victory over challenges.

Reflecting on Progress

Musical Elements: Subdued Dynamics: Transition to quieter dynamics and reflective melodies for moments of introspection.

Arpeggiated Patterns: Use gentle arpeggios to convey a reflective and contemplative mood.

Example: After the triumph, introduce a section with softer dynamics and fingerstyle arpeggios. This part represents a moment of reflection on the progress made and the lessons learned.

Reaching Milestones

Musical Elements: Fanfare-like Flourishes: Incorporate celebratory and fanfare-like motifs to signify reaching significant milestones.

Upbeat Rhythms: Use lively and upbeat rhythms to convey a sense of accomplishment and joy.

Example: Design a section with energetic strumming patterns and upbeat chord progressions, accompanied by celebratory melodic motifs. This part signifies the joy and satisfaction of achieving milestones.

Continued Exploration

Musical Elements: Modulations and Key Changes: Experiment with modulations or key changes to symbolize ongoing growth and exploration.

Varied Instrumentation: Introduce different guitar techniques or additional instruments for a diverse sonic palette.

Example: Explore new musical territories by modulating to a different key and incorporating varied guitar techniques. This section represents the continued exploration and evolution of the journey.

Final Resolution

Musical Elements: Full Chord Resonance: Conclude with full and resonant chord progressions to signify a sense of completion.

Gentle Fade-Out: Gradually fade out the music for a gentle and contemplative conclusion.

Example: Bring the composition to a close with a series of full, harmonious chords, gradually fading away. This final resolution represents the completion of the journey and the fulfillment of the initial inspiration.

By carefully considering these musical elements and structuring your guitar composition to reflect the stages of a journey, you can create a narrative-driven piece that emotionally engages the listener and tells a compelling story. Experimenting with different techniques, dynamics, and chord progressions allows you to convey the diverse experiences encountered along the way, making your composition a vivid representation of the journey's emotional landscape.

CAN I CREATE A MUSICAL THEME FOR EACH ASPIRATION?

Break down your aspirations into distinct themes. Can you create a musical theme for each aspiration, allowing the different themes to interweave in your composition?

Breaking down aspirations into distinct themes for guitar composition involves identifying key elements, emotions, or concepts associated with your aspirations and translating them into musical expressions. Themes in guitar composition serve as the foundation for conveying specific ideas and emotions throughout the piece.

Identify Core Emotions

Idea: Pinpoint the core emotions associated with your aspirations. Consider whether your journey is characterized by joy, determination, reflection, or a combination of various emotions.

Example Theme: If your aspiration revolves around personal growth, the theme could be characterized by a sense of determination and perseverance.

Explore Symbolic Imagery

Idea: Look for symbolic imagery or metaphors related to your aspirations. These can be visual or conceptual elements that resonate with your journey.

Example Theme: If your aspiration is symbolized by a mountain climb, the theme may include ascending melodies, climbing chord progressions, and dynamic shifts to mirror the challenges and triumphs of the climb.

Consider Motivations and Influences

Idea: Reflect on the motivations and influences driving your aspirations. These could be personal values, role models, or external factors shaping your journey.

Example Theme: If your aspiration is inspired by a particular cultural influence, incorporate elements of that culture's musical style into the composition, creating a thematic connection.

Delineate Narrative Elements

Idea: Break down your aspirations into distinct narrative elements or phases. Consider the beginning, middle, and end of your journey, and the emotions associated with each phase.

Example Theme: If your aspiration involves overcoming obstacles, the composition could feature a distinct theme for the challenges faced, with tense chord progressions and dynamic contrasts, transitioning to a triumphant theme for overcoming those challenges.

Explore Visualizations

Idea: Visualize the imagery associated with your aspirations. Consider how the scenery, landscapes, or visuals of your journey can be translated into musical themes.

Example Theme: If your aspiration is connected to a serene beach scene, the theme might include gentle arpeggios, relaxed chord progressions, and soothing melodies to evoke the calm and beauty of the beach.

Capture Personal Growth

Idea: Focus on themes related to personal growth and development. Consider how your aspirations reflect changes within yourself and use musical elements to capture that evolution.

Example Theme: If your aspiration involves self-discovery, create a theme that starts with introspective and contemplative elements, gradually evolving into more confident and assertive musical expressions.

Emphasize Milestones and Achievements

Idea: Highlight specific milestones or achievements associated with your aspirations. Create distinct musical themes to represent these significant moments.

Example Theme: If your aspiration involves reaching a milestone, compose a theme that features celebratory and triumphant elements to signify the accomplishment.

Connect with Cultural Influences

Idea: If your aspirations are influenced by a particular culture, incorporate musical elements from that culture into your composition to create a thematic **link**.

Example Theme: If your aspiration is tied to a cultural celebration, integrate rhythmic patterns, instruments, or scales associated with that celebration into the theme.

Reflect on Setbacks and Learning

Idea: Acknowledge setbacks and moments of learning within your aspirations. Create themes that convey resilience, reflection, and the transformative nature of setbacks.

Example Theme: If your aspiration involves overcoming failures, develop a theme that includes moments of tension, followed by resolutions and introspective passages to symbolize the learning process.

Express Gratitude and Reflection

Idea: Consider themes related to gratitude and reflection on the journey. Use musical elements to express thankfulness and appreciation for the experiences gained.

Example Theme: If your aspiration involves gratitude for support, compose a theme that exudes warmth, featuring harmonious chords and expressive melodies to convey a sense of appreciation.

ELEMENTS TO INCLUDE IN YOUR MUSICAL DIARY

If visual elements, such as sketches or images, inspire you, incorporate them into your diary. Visual cues can stimulate creative thinking and add layers to your musical ideas.

Incorporating visual elements into your musical diary for guitar composition can enhance your creative process and provide additional layers of inspiration.

MUSICAL NOTATION

Include musical notation in your diary to document specific melodies, chords, or progressions. Even if you're not fluent in traditional notation, simple tablature or chord diagrams can serve as a visual guide.

Using tablature (tabs) and chord diagrams in your musical diary for guitar composition is an effective way to document specific melodies, chords, and progressions visually. Tabs provide a clear representation of how to play individual notes, while chord diagrams illustrate the fingering positions for chords.

Here's how you can use these visual guides in your musical diary, along with examples:

Documenting Specific Melodies with Tablature

Idea: Use tabs to document intricate melodies, solos, or any specific sequences of notes you want to remember.

Example:

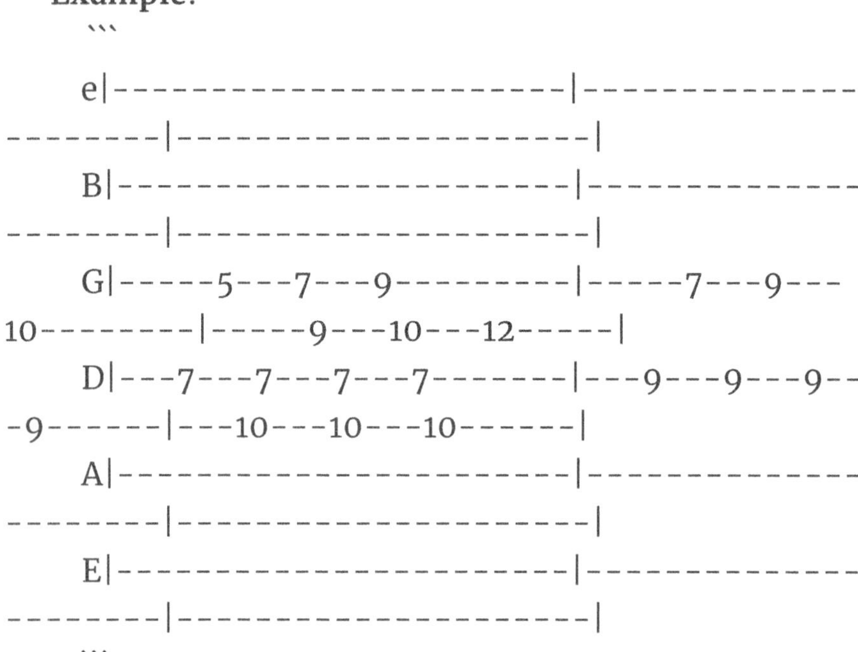

Explanation: This tab represents a portion of a melody. The numbers indicate the frets to be played on each string, providing a visual guide for recreating the melody.

Recording Chord Progressions with Chord Diagrams

Idea: Use chord diagrams to document chord progressions, ensuring you remember the voicings and transitions.

Example:
```
e|---0---|---3---|---2---|---0---|
B|---1---|---1---|---1---|---1---|
G|---0---|---0---|---2---|---2---|
D|---2---|---2---|---2---|---2---|
A|---3---|---3---|---0---|---0---|
E|-------|-------|-------|-------|
```

Explanation: This chord diagram illustrates a G major chord. Use similar diagrams to map out chord progressions, helping you remember the finger positions for each chord.

Creating Riffs and Licks with Tabs

Idea: Document catchy riffs, licks, or guitar phrases using tabs to ensure you can reproduce them later.

Example:
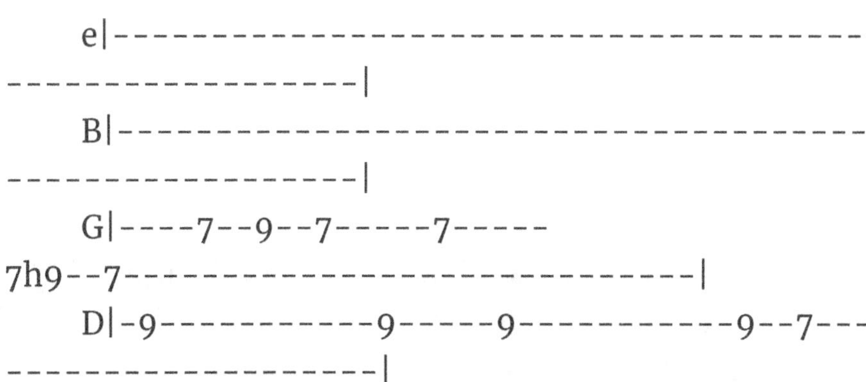
```
e|----------------------------------------------------------|
B|----------------------------------------------------------|
G|----7--9--7-----7-----7h9--7------------------------------|
D|-9-----------9-----9----------------------9--7------------|
```

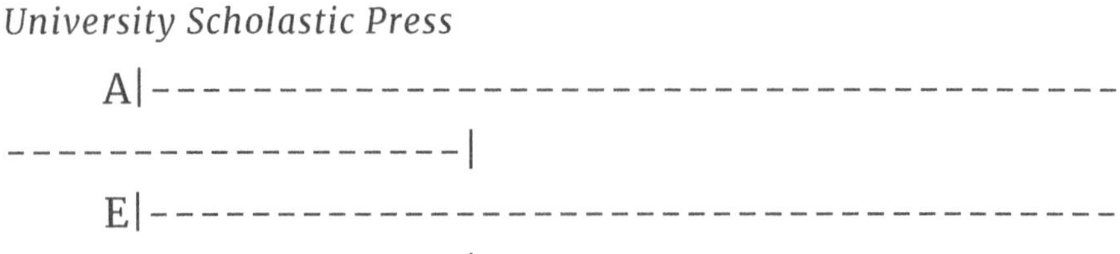

Explanation: This tab represents a short guitar riff. The numbers indicate frets, and techniques like hammer-ons (h) are used. It serves as a visual reference for playing the riff accurately.

Visualizing Arpeggios with Tabs

Idea: Document arpeggios and picking patterns using tabs to capture the nuances of your composition.
Example:

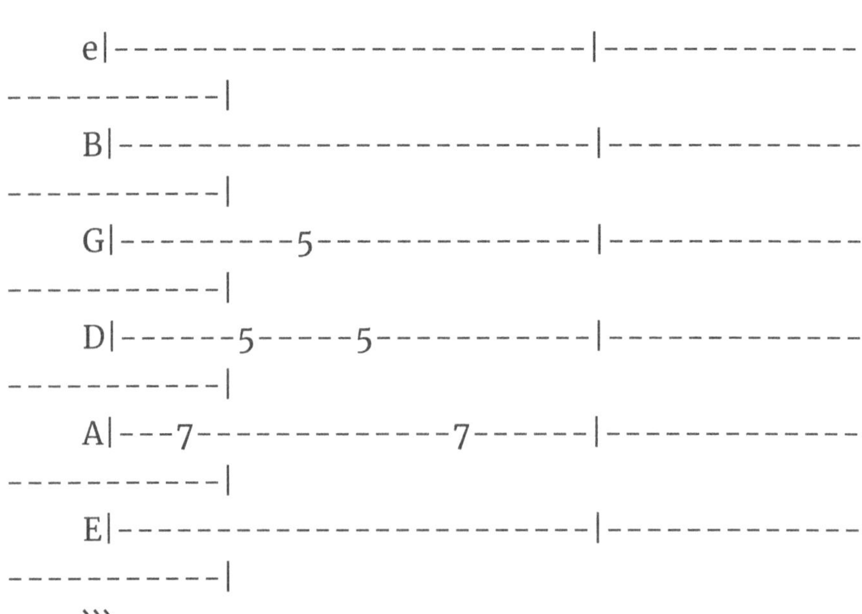

Explanation: This tab illustrates a simple arpeggio pattern. Use tabs to document various arpeggios or picking sequences in your musical diary.

Mapping Fingerstyle Patterns with Tabs

Idea: Tabs are excellent for documenting intricate fingerstyle patterns or picking techniques.
Example:

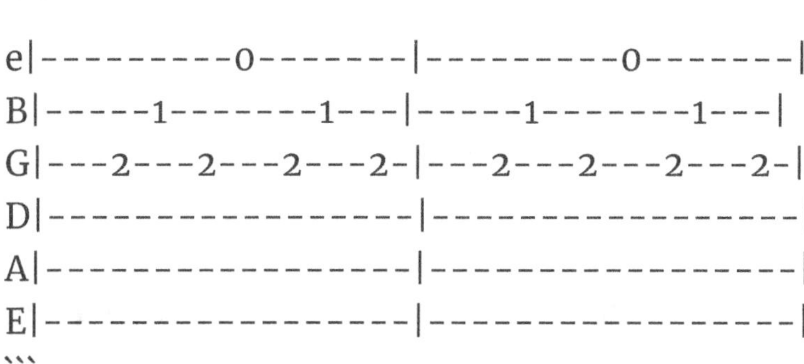

Explanation: This tab represents a basic fingerstyle pattern. Use tabs to capture the specific finger movements involved in your compositions.

Tips for Using Tabs and Chord Diagrams in Your Musical Diary

Label each tab or chord diagram with a brief description to remind yourself of the context or emotion associated with the musical idea.

Group related tabs and diagrams together to create thematic sections in your diary, such as "Melodies," "Chord Progressions," or "Fingerstyle Patterns."

Include notes or annotations to provide additional information about dynamics, articulations, or any specific techniques you want to incorporate.

By integrating tabs and chord diagrams into your musical diary, you create a visual record that facilitates easy recall and reproduction of your musical ideas. This visual aid can be particularly valuable when revisiting your compositions or collaborating with other musicians.

COLLAGE ART

Create collage art using images from magazines, photographs, or digital sources. Arrange visuals that resonate with your musical vision, conveying the atmosphere or mood you aim to capture in your composition.

Creating collage art to inspire your guitar composition and documenting it in your musical diary can be a visually engaging and imaginative process. Collages allow you to blend various elements, textures, and colors, providing a unique visual representation of the emotions and themes associated with your musical ideas.

Here's a guide on how to create collage art for inspiration, along with examples and **link**s to different collage artists for inspiration:

Steps to Create Collage Art for Musical Inspiration

Materials Needed:
Magazines, newspapers, or printed images
Photographs or printed digital images
Scissors
Glue or adhesive
Cardstock or canvas as a base

Define Themes or Emotions

Idea: Identify the themes, emotions, or concepts associated with your guitar composition. This will guide your selection of images.

Example Theme: If your composition is about nature and tranquility, collect images of landscapes, flora, and serene scenes.

Collect Visual Inspirations

Idea: Browse through magazines, online images, or your personal photo collection to gather visual inspirations that resonate with your musical themes.

Cut and Arrange

Idea: Cut out the selected images and arrange them on the base in a way that visually represents the emotions or themes you want to convey.

Example Arrangement: Combine images of a peaceful forest, a guitar, and abstract patterns to represent a composition inspired by nature and music.

Add Texture and Layers

Idea: Experiment with adding texture to your collage. This could involve layering images, incorporating textured paper, or using fabric elements.

Example Texture: Glue a piece of textured paper to represent the rough texture of tree bark or the strings of a guitar.

Incorporate Words or Lyrics

Idea: Include relevant words, lyrics, or phrases that complement the visual elements and convey the narrative or emotions of your musical composition.

Example Lyrics: If your composition has specific lyrics, incorporate them into the collage using cut-out letters or printed text.

Use Digital Tools (Optional)

Idea: If you prefer a digital approach, create a collage using graphic design software or online collage makers.

Secure and Seal

Idea: Once satisfied with the arrangement, secure the images using glue or adhesive. Consider sealing the collage with a clear varnish or adhesive spray to protect it.

Attach to Your Musical Diary

Idea: Glue or attach the completed collage to a page in your musical diary. This visual representation will serve as a constant source of inspiration.

Example Placement: Affix the collage on a page adjacent to your musical notation or written thoughts about the composition.

Inspiration from Collage Artists

Eugenia Loli:

Collage Style: Surreal and whimsical collages combining vintage imagery.

Hannah Höch:

Collage Style: A pioneer of photomontage, Höch's work explores feminism and Dadaism.

Romare Bearden:

Collage Style: Known for his collage compositions, Bearden's work often explores African American culture.

Martha Rosler:

Collage Style: Rosler's political and feminist collages challenge social norms.

These artists showcase diverse approaches to collage art, demonstrating how this medium can be a powerful form of expression and inspiration. Feel free to explore their works for ideas on composition, themes, and techniques.

Creating a collage can be a fun and personal way to visually capture the essence of your musical ideas. The combination of images, textures, and words provides a multi-sensory experience that can fuel your creativity and serve as a constant reminder of the inspiration behind your guitar compositions.

INSPIRATION BOARDS

Develop visual inspiration boards that showcase images related to your creative influences, aspirations, or the overall aesthetic you want to convey through your guitar composition. Pin or paste these boards into your diary.

Developing visual inspiration boards for your guitar composition is a wonderful way to encapsulate creative influences, aspirations, and the overall aesthetic you wish to convey. These boards serve as visual references that can spark ideas, set the mood, and provide a cohesive visual direction for your musical journey.

Steps to Develop Visual Inspiration Boards

Define Your Themes and Influences:
Identify the themes, influences, and overall aesthetic you want to convey through your guitar composition. This could include emotions, genres, cultural elements, or specific visual motifs.
Example Themes:
Nature-inspired
Vintage and nostalgic
Urban and modern

Gather Visual Elements:
Collect images, textures, colors, and patterns that resonate with your identified themes and influences. Use a variety of sources, including magazines, online image platforms, and personal photographs.

Create a Digital Collage:
Use graphic design tools or online collage makers to create a digital visual inspiration board. Arrange the collected elements in a visually appealing and cohesive manner.

Print and Cut:
Print the digital collage and cut out the individual elements. This step allows you to have tangible, physical components for your inspiration board.

Arrange on a Board or Canvas:
Arrange the printed elements on a board or canvas, creating a physical representation of your visual inspiration. Experiment with different layouts until you achieve a composition that resonates with your aesthetic.

Example Boards:
Add Personal Touches:
Enhance your visual inspiration board with personal touches such as handwritten notes, sketches, or additional elements that directly relate to your musical ideas.

Example Personal Touches:
Handwritten lyrics or quotes
Musical notations or symbols

Affix in Your Musical Diary:
Once your visual inspiration board is complete, affix it into your musical diary. Choose a dedicated section or page where it can serve as a constant source of inspiration.

Elements for Visual Inspiration Boards:

Nature-Inspired
Vintage and Nostalgic

Urban and Modern

Creating visual inspiration boards allows you to immerse yourself in the aesthetic world you want to convey through your guitar composition. These boards serve as dynamic and inspiring companions to your musical diary, encouraging creativity and enhancing the connection between your visual and musical expressions.

COLOR CODING

Use color-coding to organize and categorize different musical elements or themes. Assign specific colors to emotions, sections of your composition, or even different instruments if applicable.

Color-coding in your musical diary is a visually effective method to organize and categorize different musical elements or themes for your guitar composition. Assigning specific colors to emotions, sections of your composition, or different instruments can provide a quick and intuitive reference, making it easier to navigate and understand your musical ideas.

Steps to Use Color-Coding in Your Musical Diary

Define Categories:
Identify the categories or themes you want to color-code. This could include emotions, song sections (verse, chorus, bridge), specific instruments, or any other relevant divisions in your composition.

Example Categories:
Emotions: Joy, melancholy, excitement
Song Sections: Verse, chorus, bridge
Instruments: Guitar, vocals, percussion

Assign Colors:

Choose a color palette that resonates with the themes or elements you've defined. Assign specific colors to each category, ensuring a logical and visually distinct representation.

Example Color Assignments:

Emotions: Joy Yellow, Melancholy Blue, Excitement Red

Song Sections: Verse Green, Chorus Orange, Bridge Purple

Instruments: Guitar Brown, Vocals Pink, Percussion Gray

Create a Key:

Develop a key or legend that clearly indicates which colors correspond to each category. This key can be placed prominently in your musical diary for easy reference.

Example Key:
```

Emotions:
Joy: Yellow
Melancholy: Blue
Excitement: Red
Song Sections:
Verse: Green
Chorus: Orange
Bridge: Purple
Instruments:
Guitar: Brown
Vocals: Pink
```

Percussion: Gray
```

**Apply Color-Coding:**
Use the assigned colors to highlight or categorize different elements in your musical diary. This can include annotations, musical notations, or even visual elements like images and collages.

**Example Application:**
**Emotions**: Highlight lyrical passages expressing joy in yellow, melancholic melodies in blue, and exciting musical transitions in red.

**Song Sections**: Use designated colors to mark the beginning and end of each section, providing a visual roadmap for your composition.

**Instruments**: Color-code specific musical phrases or chords associated with each instrument.

**Maintain Consistency:**
Ensure consistency in your color-coding system throughout your musical diary. This consistency will help in quickly identifying and understanding different elements as you revisit your compositions.

**Example Consistency:**
Always use the assigned color for a specific emotion, section, or instrument to maintain clarity.

**Color Representations:**
Red: Excitement, intensity
Blue: Melancholy, calmness
Yellow: Joy, energy
Green: Freshness, verses
```

Orange: Warmth, choruses
Purple: Transition, bridges
Brown: Earthy, guitars
Pink: Vocals, expressiveness
Gray: Percussion, neutrality

Feel free to adapt the color representations based on your personal associations and preferences. The key is to establish a system that resonates with you and enhances the visual organization of your musical diary.

VISUAL REPRESENTATIONS OF DYNAMICS

Develop visual representations of dynamics, such as graphs or charts that showcase the ebb and flow of intensity in your composition. This can help you visualize the dynamic changes you want to implement.

Developing visual representations of dynamics and dynamic changes in a guitar composition can offer a unique and insightful way to showcase the ebb and flow of intensity. Visual tools like graphs or charts can help you visualize the dynamics over time, making it easier to understand the overall structure and intensity variations in your music.

Steps to Develop Visual Representations of Dynamics

Identify Dynamic Elements:
Recognize key dynamic elements in your composition, such as loud and soft passages, crescendos, decrescendos, and moments of intensity changes.

Example Dynamic Elements:

Loud sections

Soft passages

Crescendos (gradual increase in volume)

Decrescendos (gradual decrease in volume)

Peaks of intensity

Define Intensity Levels:

Assign numerical or descriptive values to represent different intensity levels in your composition. This can be subjective and based on your interpretation of the music.

Example Intensity Levels:

1: Very soft

5: Moderate

10: Very loud

Map Dynamics Over Time:

Create a timeline representing the duration of your composition. Map the intensity levels over time, indicating when dynamic changes occur.

Example Dynamic Timeline:

```

|-----1----2----3----4----5----6----7----8----9----10---|

```

Use Graphs or Charts:

Utilize graphs or charts to visually represent dynamic changes. Line graphs, bar charts, or area charts can effectively convey the intensity variations.

Example Graphs:

Line Graph: Connect intensity levels with a line over time.

Bar Chart: Use bars of varying heights to represent intensity levels at specific points.

Area Chart: Fill the area between the line and the x-axis to emphasize the dynamic range.

Color-Coding:

If you've established a color-coding system, apply it to the graph to visually enhance the representation of dynamics.

Example Color-Coding:

Use different colors for soft, moderate, and loud dynamics.

Considerations for Visual Representations

Scale: Adjust the scale of your graph to accurately reflect the dynamic changes. A larger scale can highlight subtle nuances, while a smaller scale may emphasize broader changes.

Annotations: Add annotations to your graph to explain specific dynamic events or notable sections in the composition.

Consistency: Maintain consistency with your color-coding system if you're using one. This helps create a cohesive visual language in your musical diary.

Instrumentation: If your composition involves multiple instruments, consider creating separate graphs for each instrument or grouping them in a single graph for a comprehensive view.

Application in Your Musical Diary

Affix the visual representations of dynamics in your musical diary alongside other notations, lyrics, or visual elements. This provides a holistic view of how intensity changes align with different sections of your composition.

Visualizing dynamics can enhance your understanding of the emotional arc and energy fluctuations in your guitar composition. It serves as a valuable tool for both personal reflection and collaborative discussions with other musicians.

MIND MAPS

Create mind maps that visually connect different musical ideas, themes, or influences. Use branches and nodes to illustrate the relationships between various elements in your composition.

Creating mind maps is an effective way to visually connect different musical ideas, themes, or influences in your guitar composition. Mind maps use branches and nodes to illustrate relationships between various elements, providing a clear and organized representation of the interconnected aspects of your composition.

Steps to Create Mind Maps for Guitar Composition

Identify Key Elements:
Determine the key musical ideas, themes, or influences you want to explore in your guitar composition. This could include melodic motifs, lyrical themes, emotional elements, or external influences.

Start with a Central Node:

Begin your mind map with a central node that represents the core theme or concept of your guitar composition. This central node serves as the focal point from which branches extend.

Create Branches for Elements:

Branch out from the central node to create separate branches for each key element. These elements could include lyrics, melodies, rhythms, and any other components you want to explore.

Use Nodes for Details:

Add nodes to each branch to provide details or sub-elements related to the main categories. For example, under the "Melody" branch, you might have nodes for specific melodic phrases or motifs.

Connect Related Elements:

Use connecting lines or branches to illustrate relationships between different elements. For instance, connect nodes representing lyrics to nodes representing specific musical sections where those lyrics are applied.

Color-Coding:

Consider color-coding branches or nodes to visually distinguish between different types of elements. This adds clarity and makes it easier to identify specific categories.

Add Notes and Annotations:

Include notes or annotations within nodes to provide additional context, ideas, or thoughts associated with each musical element. This can serve as a reference when revisiting your mind map.

Expand as Needed:

Expand your mind map as your composition evolves. As you develop new ideas or discover additional influences, add new branches and nodes to capture the evolving nature of your guitar composition.

Mind Mapping Software and Apps

MindMeister

Cost: Free with limited features; Premium plans available.

Features: Collaborative mind mapping, real-time collaboration, export options.

XMind

Cost: Free version available; Pro version with additional features.

Features: Various map structures, Gantt chart view, presentation mode.

Coggle

Cost: Free with limited features; Premium plans available.

Features: Real-time collaboration, unlimited public diagrams, export options.

MindMup

Cost: Free with basic features; Gold membership for additional features.

Features: Google Drive integration, collaboration, various map layouts.

Biggerplate

Cost: Free with basic features; Pro subscription for additional features.

Features: Online mind map library, community sharing, templates.

SimpleMind

Cost: Free version available; Pro version for additional features.

Features: Cross-**platform**, sync with cloud services, presentation mode.

Tips for Using Mind Maps in Guitar Composition

Flexibility: Mind maps allow for flexibility and can be adapted as your composition progresses. Feel free to add, modify, or rearrange elements as needed.

Collaboration: Some mind mapping tools support collaboration, making it possible to work on a mind map with bandmates or collaborators in real-time.

Visual Appeal: Use visual elements like icons, images, or color-coding to enhance the visual appeal of your mind map and make it more engaging.

Regular Updates: Periodically revisit and update your mind map as your composition evolves. This ensures that it remains a relevant and comprehensive representation of your creative process.

Creating mind maps for your guitar composition provides a visual roadmap that can inspire, organize, and guide your creative process. It's a versatile tool that allows you to explore the interconnected elements of your music in a dynamic and visually appealing format.

WATERCOLOR OR ARTISTIC BACKGROUNDS

Experiment with watercolor backgrounds or other artistic backgrounds for your entries. The visual aesthetics can evoke specific emotions and contribute to the overall ambiance of your creative reflections.

Experimenting with watercolor backgrounds or other artistic backgrounds in your musical diary entries can add a visually expressive and emotive dimension to your creative reflections. The visual aesthetics of these backgrounds can evoke specific emotions and contribute to the overall ambiance of your entries, enhancing the connection between visual and musical expressions.

Steps to Experiment with Watercolor Backgrounds

Select Quality Materials:
Choose high-quality watercolor paper or sketchbooks to ensure the best results for your backgrounds. Quality materials enhance the absorption and blending of watercolors.

Gather Watercolor Supplies:
Collect a variety of watercolor paints, brushes, and water containers. Experiment with different brush sizes and techniques to create diverse textures and effects.

Prep the Surface:
Wet the paper slightly before applying watercolors. This allows the colors to blend more smoothly and creates a softer background.

Experiment with Techniques:
Try various watercolor techniques such as wet-on-wet, wet-on-dry, splattering, and layering to

achieve different textures and effects. Each technique contributes to a unique visual outcome.

Blend Colors and Create Gradients:

Blend different colors to create gradients that transition smoothly across the background. Experiment with complementary or analogous color schemes to evoke specific moods.

Add Texture and Details:

Enhance your background by adding texture or details using techniques like salt sprinkling, sponging, or lifting color with a dry brush. These methods create visual interest and depth.

Let It Dry:

Allow the watercolor background to dry completely before adding any additional elements or writing in your musical diary. This ensures that the colors set properly and won't smudge.

Incorporate Inspirational Elements:

Consider incorporating inspirational elements related to your musical ideas, such as musical notes, instruments, or abstract patterns. This personalizes the background and ties it to your creative process.

Protect Pages if Necessary:

If you're using a bound diary, consider placing a protective sheet between pages to prevent the watercolor from transferring to adjacent entries.

Tips for Watercolor Backgrounds

Experiment with Color Harmonies: Explore color harmonies such as analogous, complementary, or triadic schemes to create visually appealing and harmonious backgrounds.

Incorporate White Space: Leave some areas of the paper untouched for white space. This can enhance contrast and allow other elements on the page to stand out.

Use Watercolor Pencils or Markers: For more control, consider using watercolor pencils or markers. These tools offer precision while still allowing you to achieve watercolor effects.

Practice on Scrap Paper: Before applying watercolors to your diary, practice different techniques on scrap paper to refine your skills and experiment with color combinations.

By integrating watercolor backgrounds into your musical diary, you not only enhance the visual appeal of your entries but also create a multisensory experience that reflects the emotions and ambiance of your creative process. The fluidity and unpredictability of watercolors can mirror the dynamic nature of music, adding an extra layer of artistic expression to your reflections.

TIME-LAPSE VISUALS

Incorporate time-lapse visuals that show the progression of your composition. This could be a series of sketches or images capturing different stages of your creative process.

Incorporating time-lapse visuals that show the progression of guitar composition in your musical diary can be a compelling and inspirational addition. Time-lapse visuals provide a condensed and dynamic view of your creative process, offering a unique perspective on the evolution of your musical ideas.

Steps to Incorporate Time-Lapse Visuals

Set Up a Recording Setup:
Position a camera or smartphone to capture your workspace, including your guitar, musical notations, and any other creative tools you use. Ensure good lighting for clear visuals.

Select Recording Time Intervals:
Decide on time intervals for recording segments of your composition process. This could range from every few minutes to significant milestones in your creative journey.

Record Your Composition Process:
Start recording as you work on your guitar composition. Play, write, and create as you normally would while the camera captures the progression of your musical ideas.

Edit the Time-Lapse Video:
Use video editing software to compile and speed up the recorded footage. Adjust the speed to create a time-lapse effect, condensing the entire composition process into a shorter, visually engaging video.

Incorporate Into Your Diary:
Embed or **link** the time-lapse video into your musical diary entries. This could be done digitally if your diary is online, or you can affix a QR code that **links** to the video if your diary is physical.

Add Annotations or Commentary:

Consider adding annotations or commentary to specific moments in the time-lapse video. Explain your thought process, challenges faced, or breakthroughs achieved during different phases of composition.

Reflect and Learn:

Review the time-lapse visuals periodically. Reflect on your creative process, identify patterns, and observe the growth and development of your musical ideas. Use this insight to inform future compositions.

Importance and Inspiration of Time-Lapse Visuals

Documenting Progression: Time-lapse visuals serve as a visual documentation of the progression of your guitar composition. It allows you to see how your ideas evolve over time, providing a comprehensive view of your creative journey.

Inspiration for Others: Sharing time-lapse visuals with others can be inspiring. Fellow musicians, fans, or collaborators can witness the dedication, effort, and creativity that go into your compositions, fostering a sense of connection and inspiration.

Encouraging Consistency: Regularly recording time-lapse visuals can encourage consistency in your creative practice. The act of documenting and reviewing your progress can motivate you to maintain a steady and evolving musical diary.

Examples of Time-Lapse Visuals:

Example 1: Composition Sketch to Full Song

!\[Composition Progression\](https://i.imgur.com/Bu9BnKu.gif)

This time-lapse visual showcases the transformation of a rough composition sketch into a fully developed song. It highlights the iterative process of refining and expanding musical ideas.

Example 2: Lyric Writing Time-Lapse

`![Lyric Writing Progression](https://i.imgur.com/qoIbYoZ.gif)`

A time-lapse video capturing the progression of lyric writing. The video condenses the creation of verses, choruses, and revisions, providing a captivating view of the lyric-writing process.

Tips for Time-Lapse Visuals

Experiment with Speed: Adjust the speed of your time-lapse video to find the right balance. A faster speed can condense the process, while a slightly slower speed allows viewers to discern details.

Include Commentary: If possible, add voiceover commentary or text annotations to explain key moments, decisions, or challenges faced during the composition process.

Share on Social Media: Consider sharing snippets of your time-lapse visuals on social media **platform**s. This can engage your audience and provide a sneak peek into your creative world.

Maintain Consistency: Make time-lapse recordings a regular part of your creative routine. Consistency in documenting your progress allows for a comprehensive and insightful compilation over time.

Incorporating time-lapse visuals into your musical diary not only enhances the documentation of your creative process but also adds a dynamic and visually engaging layer to your reflections. The condensed narrative of your composition journey can inspire both yourself and others, fostering a deeper appreciation for the creative effort that goes into crafting musical compositions.

TEXTURE AND FABRIC SAMPLES

Attach small fabric or texture samples to your diary. The tactile experience of different materials can evoke sensory associations and add a unique dimension to your creative reflections.

The importance of tactile inspiration in a musical diary for guitar composition lies in the power of sensory experiences to evoke emotions, memories, and unique creative reflections. Attaching small fabric or texture samples to your musical diary adds a tangible and tactile dimension to your creative process. The tactile experience of different materials can evoke sensory associations, enriching your connection with the music-making process.

Importance of Tactile Inspiration

Sensory Engagement:
Tactile experiences engage multiple senses, creating a richer and more immersive creative environment. The sense of touch adds depth to your musical reflections, making the process more personal and memorable.

Emotional Connection:
Different textures can evoke specific emotions or memories. By incorporating tactile elements, you create

a bridge between the physical world and the emotional landscape of your musical compositions.

Stimulating Creativity:

The act of touching and feeling different materials can stimulate creative thinking. It encourages a hands-on approach to composition, allowing you to explore textures that may inspire new musical ideas or themes.

Enhancing Memory Recall:

Tactile experiences are often associated with stronger memory recall. The textures you touch during your creative process can become anchors for remembering specific moments, insights, or breakthroughs in your guitar compositions.

Customizing Your Creative Space:

Adding tactile elements allows you to customize your creative space. The materials you choose can reflect the aesthetic or mood of your musical journey, creating a personalized and inspiring atmosphere.

Incorporating Fabric or Texture Samples

Choose a Variety of Materials:

Collect small samples of fabrics, textures, or materials that resonate with you. These could include silk, velvet, leather, wood, or any material that elicits a specific sensory response.

Attach Samples to Diary Pages:

Affix the small fabric or texture samples directly onto your musical diary pages. Use glue, adhesive tape, or create small pockets to hold the samples securely.

Label or Annotate:

Label each texture or fabric sample to note its significance or the emotions it evokes. Annotate how you envision incorporating these tactile elements into your guitar composition.

Experiment with Combinations:

Combine different textures on a single page to experiment with how the tactile sensations interact. Consider how these combinations might inspire nuanced musical expressions.

Create a Sensory Map:

Form a sensory map within your musical diary by arranging samples spatially. Group materials that share similar qualities or use them to represent different sections of a composition.

Tips for Tactile Inspiration

Consider Temperature: Explore materials with different temperature associations. For example, metal may feel cool, while wool might feel warm. This can add another layer to the sensory experience.

Rotate Samples Periodically: To keep the tactile experience fresh, consider rotating or introducing new texture samples periodically. This ensures that your sensory exploration remains dynamic and evolving.

Combine with Visual Elements: Pair tactile samples with visual elements such as color-coded annotations or drawings to create a multisensory representation of your creative process.

Reflect in Writing: Write reflections or thoughts alongside the tactile samples. Describe how each texture influences your creative mindset or sparks specific musical ideas.

Incorporating tactile inspiration into your musical diary for guitar composition creates a multisensory experience that goes beyond traditional notations. The act of touching and feeling different materials enriches your creative reflections, adding a unique and personal dimension to your musical journey.

Remember, the visual elements you choose should resonate with your personal style and enhance your connection to the music you're creating. Feel free to experiment with different mediums and find a visual language that complements your musical journey.

REVIEW AND REFLECT PERIODICALLY

Set aside time periodically to review and reflect on your entries. This allows you to observe patterns, notice recurring themes, and gain a deeper understanding of your creative process.

Periodically reviewing and reflecting on your entries in the musical diary for guitar composition is a valuable practice for gaining insights, tracking progress, and refining your creative process.

Here are some questions to ask yourself during these review sessions:

What Were the Initial Sparks of Inspiration for Each Entry?

Reflect on the sources of inspiration for each entry. Were they specific experiences, emotions, or external stimuli? Understanding the origins can provide clarity on your creative triggers.

Have New Ideas Emerged from Previous Entries?

Assess whether new ideas or variations have emerged from previous entries. How has your initial inspiration evolved, and are there unexpected directions your composition has taken?

Which Entries Elicited Strong Emotional Responses?

Identify entries that elicited strong emotional responses. These could be moments of joy, frustration, or surprise. Understanding the emotional impact of your ideas can guide future creative decisions.

How Have Your Musical Techniques Evolved or Developed?

Evaluate the evolution of your guitar techniques. Have you experimented with new fingerpicking patterns, chord voicings, or rhythmic elements? Consider how these developments contribute to the overall texture of your composition.

How Has Your Composition Evolved Over Time?

Examine the overall progression of your composition. How has it evolved from the initial concept to its current state? Identify key milestones and transformations in your creative journey.

Have You Achieved Specific Goals Set in Previous Entries?

Review any specific goals or objectives set in previous entries. Have you achieved them, or have your goals evolved along with your creative process?

What Challenges Have You Encountered, and How Were They Addressed?

Reflect on challenges encountered during the composition process. How did you address these challenges, and what did you learn from overcoming them? Challenges often lead to valuable insights and growth.

Are There Surprises or Unintended Developments That Enhanced the Composition?

Acknowledge any surprises or unintended developments that enhanced your composition. Creativity often brings unexpected twists, and recognizing and embracing these can lead to unique and compelling outcomes.

Are There Unexplored Ideas or Concepts Worth Revisiting?

Identify any unexplored ideas or concepts in previous entries that may be worth revisiting. Your diary may contain hidden gems that could contribute to the richness of your composition.

Are You Still Aligned with the Initial Purpose or Concept?

Revisit the initial purpose or concept of your composition. Does it still align with your current creative vision, or have your goals and intentions evolved?

How Has External Feedback Influenced Your Creative Choices?

If you've received external feedback, consider how it has influenced your creative choices. Have you incorporated constructive feedback, and how has it shaped the direction of your composition?

How Has Your Relationship with Your Composition Evolved?

Reflect on the evolving relationship between you and your composition. How has your connection to the music deepened, and in what ways have you grown as a musician and creator?

What Have You Learned About Your Creative Process?

Assess what you've learned about your creative process. Are there specific habits, rituals, or approaches that have proven particularly effective or challenging?

What Excites You Most About Continuing This Composition?

Conclude your reflection by identifying what excites you most about continuing your composition. Is there a particular aspect or potential outcome that fuels your enthusiasm?

What Specific Actions Will You Take Based on Your Reflections?

Translate your reflections into actionable steps. What specific actions will you take based on your assessments? Outline a plan for the next phase of your composition process.

By asking these questions during your periodic reviews, you create a structured approach to understanding your creative journey, fostering growth, and refining your guitar composition with each reflection.

Experiment with Unconventional Ideas

Encourage yourself to jot down unconventional or experimental ideas. Your musical diary is a safe space to explore uncharted territory and push the boundaries of your creativity.

Experimenting with unconventional ideas in your musical diary for guitar composition can lead to unique and innovative results.

Found Object Instruments

Experiment with creating instruments from found objects. Incorporate unconventional materials, such as kitchen utensils, household items, or even natural objects, to produce distinctive sounds. Document how these found object instruments influence your composition.

Experimenting with creating instruments from found objects is a creative and resourceful way to explore unique sounds and textures in your guitar compositions. Found object instruments can add an unconventional and distinctive element to your musical palette.

Experimenting with Found Object Instruments

Selecting Found Objects:
Explore your surroundings for objects with interesting shapes, materials, or textures. Look for items that produce distinct sounds when struck, shaken, or manipulated.

Functional Criteria:
Consider the functionality of the found object. It should be durable enough to withstand playing, and its

shape or structure should allow for sound production. Objects with resonant qualities are particularly interesting.

Sound Exploration:

Experiment with how each found object produces sound. Tap, shake, or bow the object to discover its sonic potential. Pay attention to the pitch, volume, and timbre of the sounds it generates.

Modify and Enhance:

Modify the found objects to enhance their musical qualities. This could involve attaching strings, adding resonators, or altering the shape to achieve desired tones. Be open to unconventional modifications.

Combine Objects:

Combine multiple found objects to create hybrid instruments. Experiment with how different materials and shapes interact to produce a unique sonic blend.

Construction Considerations:

Ensure that the construction of your found object instrument allows for stability and playability. Consider attaching handles, creating playing surfaces, or incorporating mechanisms for sound modulation.

Examples of Functional Found Object Instruments:

Example 1: The Thumb Piano (Kalimba)

Materials Needed:

A flat piece of wood or a small box

Metal tines or wooden strips of varying lengths

Screws or bolts

Construction Steps:

Attach the metal tines or wooden strips to the wooden base using screws or bolts.

Tune each tine to a specific pitch by adjusting its length.

Play the thumb piano by plucking the tines with your thumbs.

Example 2: Percussive Shakers

Materials Needed:

Small, empty containers (e.g., pill bottles, film canisters)

Small beads, rice, or seeds

Strong adhesive or tape

Construction Steps:

Fill the containers with beads, rice, or seeds.

Seal the containers tightly.

Attach the containers to a wooden or plastic handle using adhesive or tape.

Shake the shakers to produce rhythmic percussion sounds.

Example 3: Glass Bottle Xylophone

Materials Needed:

Glass bottles of varying sizes

Water

Wooden or metal mallets

Construction Steps:

Fill each glass bottle with a different amount of water to create varied pitches.

Arrange the bottles in a row or cluster.

Play the xylophone by striking the bottles with mallets.

Tips for Creating Found Object Instruments

Experiment with Tuning: Explore ways to tune your found object instruments. This could involve adjusting lengths, adding or removing materials, or altering the tension of attached elements.

Combine with Traditional Instruments: Integrate your found object instruments into your guitar compositions by combining them with traditional instruments. This juxtaposition can create a unique and eclectic sonic landscape.

Document Your Creations: Record and document the sounds produced by your found object instruments. This documentation can serve as a reference for future compositions and arrangements.

Be Open to Improvisation: Found object instruments often lend themselves to improvisation. Embrace the spontaneity and unpredictability of these creations, allowing them to influence the direction of your musical compositions.

Creating functional instruments from found objects not only expands your sonic possibilities but also adds an element of resourcefulness and ingenuity to your creative process. These unique instruments can become signature elements in your guitar compositions, offering a distinctive and personal touch to your musical expression.

EXTENDED TECHNIQUES

Explore extended guitar techniques beyond traditional playing methods. This could include bowing the guitar strings, using prepared guitar techniques (attaching objects to the strings), or incorporating tapping and percussive elements.

Exploring extended guitar techniques can greatly enhance your expressive range and add unique textures to your compositions. Beyond traditional playing methods, extended techniques involve unconventional approaches and sounds produced by manipulating the instrument in innovative ways.

Here are some examples of various extended guitar techniques for composition:

Prepared Guitar

Description: Adding objects to alter the sound of the guitar.

Example: Attach paper clips or other small objects to the strings to create percussive and rattling sounds.

Harmonics

Description: Producing high-pitched tones by lightly touching the strings.

Example: Use natural harmonics by lightly touching the string above the 12th fret while plucking.

Tapping

Description: Using fingers or both hands to tap on the strings.

Example: Eddie Van Halen's two-handed tapping technique is a famous example.

Slide Guitar

Description: Sliding a smooth object (e.g., glass or metal slide) along the strings.

Example: Duane Allman's slide guitar work in "Layla" by Derek and the Dominos.

Scraping

Description: Running a hard object (e.g., pick, coin) along the strings.

Example: Creating a rhythmic scraping sound by running a coin across the strings during strumming.

Bow Techniques

Description: Using a bow (as in string instruments) on the guitar strings.

Example: Experimental guitarist Fred Frith incorporates bowing in his performances.

Feedback

Description: Allowing the guitar to produce sustained feedback by positioning it close to the amplifier.

Example: Jimi Hendrix's use of feedback in "Star–Spangled Banner."

Percussive Techniques

Description: Using the guitar body as a percussion instrument.

Example: Andy McKee's percussive fingerstyle techniques, tapping and slapping the guitar body for rhythmic effects.

Prepared Capos

Description: Placing objects under or over the strings near the frets to alter pitch or create drones.

Example: Using a pencil as a makeshift capo to create unusual chord voicings.

Alternate Tunings

Description: Changing the standard tuning to create new harmonic possibilities.

Example: Joni Mitchell's use of alternate tunings in songs like "Big Yellow Taxi."

Whammy Bar Techniques

Description: Using the whammy bar to create pitch bends and dive-bombs.

Example: Steve Vai's extensive use of the whammy bar in his virtuosic performances.

Flageolet or Pinch Harmonics

Description: Producing high-pitched squeals by lightly touching the string with the thumb after picking.

Example: Zakk Wylde's aggressive use of pinch harmonics in metal solos.

Aleatoric or Chance Techniques

Description: Introducing an element of chance or randomness into your playing.

Example: Composing sections where specific notes or effects are determined by chance (e.g., dice rolls).

Body Percussion

Description: Incorporating percussive sounds by tapping, slapping, or drumming on the guitar body.

Example: Using the guitar as both a melodic and percussive instrument simultaneously.

Fretboard Tapping

Description: Tapping on the fretboard with fingers to produce rapid and intricate patterns.

Example: Stanley Jordan's two-handed tapping technique on the fretboard.

Spectral Techniques

Description: Exploring harmonics and overtones through specific playing techniques.

Example: Composing pieces that highlight specific harmonic series or spectral components.

Electronic Manipulation

Description: Introducing electronic effects and manipulations (e.g., pedals, loopers) to transform the guitar's sound.

Example: The Edge's extensive use of effects in U2's sound.

Reverse Playing

Description: Recording guitar parts and playing them in reverse for unique textures.

Example: Jimi Hendrix's use of reverse guitar parts in "Are You Experienced."

Muted Strumming or Choking

Description: Strumming with a partially muted hand for a percussive effect.

Example: Choking the strings with the palm while strumming to create a staccato rhythm.

Glissando or Slide Techniques

Description: Sliding along the strings to create smooth pitch transitions.

Example: Creating atmospheric sounds by sliding up and down the fretboard.

Experimenting with Extended Techniques

Combine Techniques: Explore combining multiple extended techniques within a composition to create intricate and varied textures.

Improvise and Explore: Allow room for improvisation and experimentation with extended techniques during live performances or recordings.

Create New Techniques: Don't be afraid to invent your own techniques by exploring the sonic possibilities of the guitar.

Study Experimental Guitarists: Listen to and study the works of experimental guitarists who push the boundaries of traditional playing methods.

By incorporating these extended guitar techniques into your compositions, you can unlock a vast sonic palette and bring fresh and innovative elements to your music. Experimenting with these techniques not only expands your creative possibilities but also adds a distinctive and personal touch to your guitar compositions.

REVERSE ENGINEERING

Record short musical phrases or sections and reverse them. Listen to the reversed audio and identify interesting textures or melodic ideas. Use these reversed elements as inspiration for composing forward-facing sections.

Recording short musical phrases or sections and reversing them can be a creative and unconventional approach to guitar composition. Listening to the reversed audio can reveal interesting textures, unexpected harmonies, and novel melodic ideas. Using these reversed elements as inspiration for composing forward-facing sections adds a unique and experimental dimension to your musical creations.

Here's how to incorporate this technique into your guitar compositions:

Steps for Reversing Musical Phrases

Record a Short Musical Phrase:
Play a short guitar phrase or section that you find interesting or want to explore further. This could be a melodic line, a chord progression, or a combination of both.

Record and Reverse:
Record the musical phrase using a digital audio workstation (DAW) or any recording device. Once recorded, reverse the audio clip to play it backward.

Listen and Analyze:
Take time to listen to the reversed audio. Pay attention to the new textures, harmonies, and sonic characteristics that emerge. Note any elements that stand out or inspire you.

Identify Interesting Elements:
Identify specific moments, tones, or transitions in the reversed audio that captivate your ear. These could be unique timbres, unexpected harmonies, or reversed articulations.

Use as Inspiration:
Draw inspiration from the reversed elements to compose new forward-facing sections. This might involve incorporating reversed motifs, building complementary melodies, or adapting harmonic structures.

Examples of Reversed Guitar Composition:
Example 1: Reversed Chord Progression Inspiration

Original Recording:

A simple chord progression (e.g., C major to G major).

Reversed Audio:

The reversed version of the chord progression.

Inspiration for Forward-Facing Section:

Utilize the reversed version's unexpected transitions to inspire a new chord progression in the forward-facing section. Experiment with inversions and voicings influenced by the reversed harmony.

Example 2: Melodic Fragment Transformation

Original Recording:

A short melodic fragment played on the guitar.

Reversed Audio:

The reversed version of the melodic fragment.

Inspiration for Forward-Facing Section:

Extract melodic motifs from the reversed audio and adapt them to create a unique melody in the forward-facing section. Experiment with rhythmic variations inspired by the reversed timing.

Tips for Reversed Guitar Composition

Experiment with Different Phrases: Try reversing various types of musical phrases, including chord progressions, arpeggios, or percussive elements. Each type of phrase may yield different and interesting results.

Layer Reversed and Original Elements: Blend reversed elements with the original forward-facing sections to create a dynamic and evolving composition.

This can add depth and complexity to your musical arrangement.

Apply Effects Sparingly: Experiment with subtle effects, such as reverb or delay, on the reversed audio to enhance its atmospheric qualities. Be mindful not to overwhelm the composition with effects.

Record Multiple Takes: Record multiple takes of different phrases and experiment with reversing each one. This allows you to explore a variety of sonic possibilities and choose the most compelling elements.

Incorporating reversed musical elements into your guitar compositions offers a fresh perspective and opens the door to unexpected sonic landscapes. By embracing this technique, you can add a layer of intrigue and experimentation to your creative process, ultimately leading to compositions that showcase a unique blend of forward and reversed musical elements.

GRAPHIC NOTATION

Explore graphic notation as a means of expressing musical ideas visually. Use drawings, symbols, or abstract shapes to represent musical elements, allowing for a more open and interpretive approach to composition.

Exploring graphic notation can be a fascinating and expressive way to visually represent musical ideas for your guitar composition. Graphic notation involves using drawings, symbols, or abstract shapes to convey musical elements, providing a more open and interpretive approach to composition.

Let's dive into graphic notation for guitar composition:

Steps to Explore Graphic Notation

Understand Basic Graphic Notation Elements:
Familiarize yourself with basic graphic notation symbols. These can include lines, shapes, and symbols representing various musical parameters such as pitch, dynamics, and rhythm.

Create Your Graphic Notation System:
Develop your personal graphic notation system or experiment with existing ones. Consider how you want to represent pitch, duration, intensity, and other musical elements visually.

Experiment with Abstract Shapes:
Use abstract shapes to represent different musical elements. For example, circles might represent sustained tones, jagged lines could denote staccato articulations, and varying sizes of shapes may indicate dynamics.

Combine Symbols and Drawings:
Combine symbols and drawings to convey nuanced musical instructions. For instance, a symbol for tremolo combined with a wavy line might represent a fluctuating dynamic.

Embrace Interpretation:
Graphic notation encourages interpretation. Embrace the idea that performers will bring their own understanding to your visual notations, allowing for a more collaborative and unique performance.

Examples of Graphic Notation Elements:

Example 1: Pitch Representation
Notation Element:
Circles at different heights on a vertical line.
Interpretation:
Each circle represents a pitch, and its vertical placement indicates the pitch's height.
Example 2: Rhythmic Articulation
Notation Element:
A series of jagged lines intersecting a curved line.
Interpretation:
The jagged lines represent staccato articulations, while the curved line indicates a legato passage.
Example 3: Dynamic Intensity
Notation Element:
Gradually increasing and decreasing sizes of triangles.
Interpretation:
The size of the triangles corresponds to dynamic intensity, with larger triangles indicating louder passages and smaller triangles representing softer sections.

Online Resources for Graphic Notation Elements

OpenMusicTheory Graphic Notation Elements
This resource provides a collection of graphic notation elements with explanations of their meanings. It serves as a useful reference for incorporating graphic notation into your compositions.
Composing with Color Graphic Notation Symbols

This website offers visual representations of various graphic notation symbols, allowing you to explore and incorporate unique elements into your compositions.

Tips for Exploring Graphic Notation

Be Consistent: Establish a consistent set of symbols or shapes to maintain clarity in your notation system. Consistency helps performers understand and interpret your visual language.

Combine with Traditional Notation: If you're using graphic notation extensively, consider combining it with traditional notation to provide a balance between specificity and interpretive freedom.

Experiment with Color: Introduce color to your graphic notation elements to convey additional information or emotional nuances. Color can enhance the visual impact of your notations.

Collaborate with Performers: Engage in discussions with performers to ensure mutual understanding of your graphic notations. Collaborative input can lead to a more successful realization of your intended musical ideas.

Exploring graphic notation opens up new possibilities for expressing your musical ideas visually. By developing a personalized notation system and experimenting with abstract shapes, you can create compositions that invite interpretation and engage performers in a unique and visually rich musical experience.

Interactive Elements

Integrate interactive elements into your composition. This could involve incorporating sensors, MIDI controllers, or other technology to allow for audience interaction or real-time manipulation of your guitar sounds.

Incorporating sensors, MIDI controllers, or other technology into your guitar composition can add a dynamic and interactive element, allowing for audience interaction or real-time manipulation of your guitar sounds.

MIDI Controllers

Description: MIDI controllers allow you to interface with digital devices and software, expanding your creative possibilities.

Examples:

Behringer FCB1010 MIDI Foot Controller: A versatile foot controller with multiple switches and expression pedals, suitable for hands-free operation.

Keith McMillen Instruments SoftStep 2: A flexible and programmable foot controller with pressure-sensitive pads for expressive control.

Touch and Pressure Sensors

Description: Touch and pressure sensors respond to physical contact, enabling hands-on control of various parameters.

Examples:

Makey Makey: A simple and affordable kit that turns everyday objects into touchpads, allowing you to trigger MIDI events by touching different surfaces.

Sensel Morph: A versatile touch-sensitive interface with interchangeable overlays, offering a range of tactile experiences for expressive control.

Gesture Controllers

Description: Gesture controllers detect movements and gestures, providing a unique way to interact with your guitar sounds.

Examples:

Leap Motion Controller: Tracks hand movements in 3D space, allowing for gesture-based control of virtual instruments or effects.

Myo Gesture Control Armband: An armband that detects muscle movements, translating gestures into control signals for music software.

Interactive Floor Controllers

Description: Floor controllers that respond to footsteps or pressure, offering an interactive element during performances.

Examples:

ROLI Seaboard RISE: An expressive MIDI controller with a soft, pressure-sensitive surface that allows for unique playing techniques and interaction.

ROLI BLOCKS: Modular, touch-sensitive blocks that can be combined for interactive control and performance.

Arduino-Based Solutions

Description: Arduino allows you to create custom electronic interfaces for your guitar, tailored to your specific needs.

Examples:

Arduino Uno: A widely used microcontroller **platform** that can be programmed to interface with sensors, switches, and other electronic components.

Adafruit Capacitive Touch Sensor Breakout MPR121: An example of a touch sensor breakout board that can be integrated into Arduino projects.

Interactive Software Platforms

Description: Software **platform**s that enable real-time manipulation and interaction with your guitar sounds.

Examples:

Max/MSP]: A visual programming language for music and multimedia, allowing you to create custom interactive patches.

TouchDesigner: A node-based visual programming language for interactive multimedia content, suitable for creating immersive guitar performances.

Tips for Implementation

Experiment and Iterate: Start by experimenting with one or two technologies and gradually incorporate more as you become familiar with the integration process.

Collaborate with Technologists: Collaborate with technologists or programmers to help you implement and refine your interactive setup.

Consider Audience Engagement: Tailor your interactive elements to enhance the audience's engagement without overshadowing the musical experience.

Cost Considerations:

Costs can vary widely based on the specific technologies and brands you choose. MIDI controllers can range from $50 to several hundred dollars, while sensors and Arduino components are often more affordable.

Integrating sensors, MIDI controllers, and other technologies into your guitar composition opens up exciting possibilities for real-time manipulation and audience interaction. By exploring these tools and experimenting with their capabilities, you can create unique and immersive musical experiences that blend traditional guitar playing with cutting-edge technology.

Ambient Soundscape Integration

Record ambient sounds from your environment and integrate them into your composition. This could include sounds from nature, cityscapes, or any other sonic elements that add a unique layer to your music.

Ambient soundscapes in guitar composition involve creating atmospheric and immersive sonic environments that go beyond traditional melodic or rhythmic elements. These soundscapes often include environmental sounds, textures, and atmospheres to evoke a particular mood or setting. Recording sounds from the environment and integrating them into guitar composition can add depth, realism, and a unique sonic character.

Let's explore creating ambient soundscapes and integrate environmental recordings into your guitar compositions:

Creating Ambient Soundscapes

Environmental Sound Recording
Capture sounds from your surroundings, such as nature, urban environments, or any interesting atmospheres.
Example: Record birdsong, rustling leaves, flowing water, city traffic, or other ambient sounds.
Layering Textures:
Layer various recorded textures to build a rich sonic landscape.
Example: Combine recordings of wind, distant traffic, and subtle echoes to create a layered ambient texture.
Manipulating Time and Space:
Experiment with time-stretching, pitch-shifting, and spatial effects to alter the perception of time and space in the soundscapes.
Example: Slow down a recorded stream to create a dreamy, elongated texture or use panning to simulate movement.
Instrumental Integration:

Blend the ambient soundscapes seamlessly with your guitar playing.

Example: Play sustained chords or individual notes on the guitar, allowing them to resonate within the ambient soundscape.

Dynamic Changes:

Introduce gradual changes or shifts in the ambient soundscape to maintain interest.

Example: Slowly introduce new environmental recordings, alter the pitch of existing elements, or change the spatial distribution.

Integrating Environmental Recordings into Guitar Composition

Recording Techniques:

Use high-quality microphones to capture environmental sounds with clarity and detail.

Example: Position microphones strategically to capture the desired sound sources and minimize unwanted noise.

Field Recording Equipment:

Invest in portable field recording equipment for on-the-go sound capture.

Example: Portable recorders like the Zoom H5 or Tascam DR-40X are suitable for capturing environmental sounds.

Editing and Processing:

Edit and process the recorded sounds to fit the desired mood or atmosphere.

Example: Apply equalization, reverb, or other effects to enhance or modify the recorded sounds.

Syncing with Guitar Playing:
Ensure that the tempo and timing of the environmental recordings align with your guitar playing.

Example: Use a digital audio workstation (DAW) to synchronize the ambient soundscape with your guitar track.

Creative Layering:
Layer the environmental recordings with your guitar performance for a cohesive and immersive blend.

Example: Integrate the sound of rain into a gentle fingerpicked acoustic guitar piece for a calming and natural atmosphere.

Guitar Compositions with Ambient Soundscapes

"Deep Blue" by Hammock:
This ambient post-rock band often integrates field recordings, such as ocean waves and distant thunder, into their guitar-driven compositions.

"Music for Airports" by Brian Eno:
Brian Eno's ambient masterpiece incorporates tape loops of various environmental sounds, creating a tranquil and reflective sonic environment.

"F#A# ∞" by Godspeed You! Black Emperor:
This post-rock band incorporates ambient field recordings, including radio broadcasts and spoken word samples, into their compositions.

Tips for Effective Integration

Attention to Detail: Pay attention to the details of the environmental recordings, such as subtle background noises and the overall sonic character.

Experimentation: Don't be afraid to experiment with unconventional sounds or manipulated recordings to achieve unique textures.

Balance: Ensure a balanced mix between the guitar and ambient elements, allowing each to complement the other without overpowering.

By carefully selecting and manipulating environmental recordings, you can create ambient soundscapes that enhance the emotional impact of your guitar compositions. The integration of these elements adds a cinematic quality, transporting listeners to immersive sonic environments that resonate with the mood and theme of your musical expression.

STORYTELLING WITH SOUND EFFECTS

Incorporate sound effects into your composition to tell a story. This could include recorded snippets of dialogue, ambient sounds, or even narrative elements conveyed through unconventional guitar techniques.

Storytelling with sound effects in guitar composition involves using a combination of musical elements and non-musical sounds to create a narrative or evoke specific emotions. These sound effects can serve as sonic elements that contribute to a larger storytelling experience. Incorporating storytelling into sound effects for guitar composition allows you to paint vivid sonic images and convey a narrative or atmosphere.

Incorporating Storytelling with Sound Effects

Selecting Relevant Sound Effects:
Choose sound effects that align with the narrative or theme of your composition.

Example: In a composition inspired by a rainy day, incorporate sound effects of raindrops, distant thunder, or ambient street sounds.

Establishing a Context:
Use sound effects to set the stage and establish the context of your musical narrative.

Example: Begin with the sound of footsteps on a gravel path to create the ambiance of someone walking through a forest before the guitar melody starts.

Creating Transitions:
Use sound effects to smoothly transition between different sections of your composition, guiding the listener through the narrative.

Example: Use the sound of a door creaking to transition from a mysterious introduction to a more upbeat and lively guitar section.

Enhancing Emotional Impact:
Integrate sound effects to enhance the emotional impact of specific moments in your composition.

Example: Incorporate sounds like laughter, birdsong, or waves crashing to evoke joy, tranquility, or excitement, respectively.

Building Atmosphere:
Layer ambient sound effects to build a rich and immersive sonic atmosphere.

Example: Combine sounds of wind, distant chatter, and rustling leaves to create the feeling of an open-air market in a guitar composition.

Examples of Guitar Compositions with Storytelling Sound Effects

"The Great Gig in the Sky" by Pink Floyd:
This classic Pink Floyd track features the haunting sound of a woman's wordless vocalizations, adding an emotional and ethereal quality to the guitar-driven piece.

"Bullet the Blue Sky" by U2:
U2's guitar-driven composition is enhanced by sound effects such as helicopters, gunfire, and distorted radio broadcasts, contributing to the song's narrative about violence and conflict.

"Every Grain of Sand" by Bob Dylan:
Bob Dylan's acoustic composition is accompanied by subtle sound effects, including bird sounds, contributing to the reflective and nature-inspired atmosphere of the song.

Tips for Effective Storytelling with Sound Effects

Subtlety is Key: Keep sound effects subtle to avoid overpowering the musical elements. They should enhance the experience without distracting from the guitar composition.

Align with Theme: Ensure that the chosen sound effects align with the overall theme or narrative you want to convey through your guitar composition.

Careful Mixing: Pay attention to the balance and mixing of sound effects to ensure they blend seamlessly with the guitar and other musical elements.

Use of Foley Sounds: Consider incorporating foley sounds, which are reproduced everyday sounds (footsteps, doors creaking, etc.), to add realism and context to your storytelling.

Implementation in a Guitar Composition

Example:

Intro:

Sound Effect: The distant sound of waves crashing on a shore.

Guitar: Begin with a slow, atmospheric guitar progression that complements the waves, setting the scene for a coastal narrative.

Verse 1:

Sound Effect: Seagulls crying in the background.

Guitar: Introduce a melodic guitar line that mirrors the seagull cries, creating a sense of unity between the natural sounds and the musical elements.

Chorus:

Sound Effect: Light rain and distant thunder.

Guitar: Shift to a more contemplative guitar section, with rain sounds creating a reflective and introspective atmosphere.

Bridge:

Sound Effect: Footsteps on a wooden pier.

Guitar: Transition to a bridge section with percussive guitar playing that mirrors the rhythmic footsteps, building anticipation for the upcoming climax.

Climax:

Sound Effect: Wind howling and a distant ship horn.

Guitar: Build the intensity of the guitar playing to match the climactic soundscape, creating a sense of drama and tension.

Outro:

Sound Effect: Waves receding, leaving a peaceful ambiance.

Guitar: Wind down the composition with a serene guitar outro, allowing the waves to subside and leaving the listener with a tranquil resolution.

Incorporating storytelling with sound effects into your guitar compositions adds a cinematic and immersive dimension, allowing you to transport listeners to specific settings or evoke powerful emotions. By carefully selecting and integrating sound effects, you can create a cohesive narrative that enhances the overall impact of your guitar compositions.

INCORPORATE NON-MUSICAL ELEMENTS

Integrate non-musical elements into your composition. This could include spoken word, poetry, or even the incorporation of visual art. Experiment with the ways these elements interact with your guitar playing.

Unusual Performance Spaces

Experiment with performing or recording in unconventional spaces. This could include outdoor environments, abandoned buildings, or any location that adds a unique acoustic quality to your guitar composition.

Algorithmic Composition

Experiment with algorithmic composition using software or programming tools. Create algorithms that generate musical patterns, and incorporate the results into your composition.

Remember, the key to experimenting with unconventional ideas is to stay open-minded and embrace the creative process. Allow yourself the freedom to explore, make mistakes, and discover new possibilities that can enrich your musical diary and, ultimately, your guitar compositions.

USING THE DIARY AS A SOURCE FOR YOUR COMPOSITION

When you embark on your guitar composition, revisit your musical diary for inspiration. Use the documented thoughts, emotions, and musical ideas as building blocks for your creative endeavor.

Using your musical diary as a source for guitar composition involves extracting inspiration, ideas, and insights from your recorded entries to inform and shape your compositions.

Explore Emotional Resonance

Pay attention to entries that evoke strong emotional responses. Consider how you can translate these emotions into musical expressions on the guitar. Emotionally charged entries can serve as a foundation for creating impactful compositions.

Extract Inspirational Quotes or Descriptions

If you've included descriptive language or quotes in your diary, extract phrases or words that evoke vivid imagery. Use these descriptions to guide the mood, atmosphere, or narrative of your guitar compositions.

Connect Entries to Themes or Concepts

Group entries that revolve around similar themes or concepts. Identify overarching ideas that can serve as the foundation for a cohesive composition. This could be based on narratives, symbolism, or personal experiences.

Experiment with Hybrid Ideas

Experiment with combining multiple ideas from different diary entries to create hybrids. This approach allows you to synthesize diverse elements and foster creativity in your guitar compositions.

Create a Conceptual Framework

Develop a conceptual framework for your composition based on the insights from your diary. Outline the structure, progression, and thematic elements that will guide your guitar composition.

Experiment with Song Structures

Experiment with different song structures inspired by your diary entries. Whether it's a traditional verse-chorus structure or a more experimental form, let the structure be influenced by the flow of your ideas.

Incorporate Feedback and Reflections

If you've documented feedback or reflections on your musical ideas, consider incorporating these insights into your compositions. Use constructive feedback as a guide for refining and enhancing your guitar work.

Set Goals for Composition Sessions

Based on your review of the musical diary, set specific goals for your composition sessions. Define what you aim to achieve in terms of structure, melody, harmony, or any other elements inspired by your diary entries.

Document Progress

As you work on your compositions, document your progress in the diary. Record insights, breakthroughs, challenges, and any adjustments made during the creative process.

Stay Open to New Directions

While your musical diary serves as a valuable guide, stay open to new directions and spontaneous ideas that may arise during the composition process. Allow for flexibility and creative exploration.

Reflect on Growth and Evolution

Periodically reflect on how your compositions have evolved based on insights from your musical diary. Consider how your growth as a musician is reflected in the development of your guitar compositions.

Celebrate Achievements

Celebrate achievements and milestones reached in your guitar compositions. Acknowledge the progress you've made and use positive experiences as motivation for future creative endeavors.

By integrating your musical diary into your composition process, you create a dynamic and interconnected relationship between reflection, documentation, and musical expression. This cyclical approach allows your creative journey to evolve and flourish over time.

Example Entry in a Musical Diary:
Date: [Insert Date]

Today, I experienced a moment of quiet introspection while walking through the park. The rustling leaves and distant chatter created a serene atmosphere that resonated deeply with me. Inspired by this, I envisioned a gentle fingerstyle melody with open chords, capturing the tranquility of that moment. The chords transition seamlessly, mirroring the ebb and flow of the breeze. This piece could become a reflection on finding solace in nature amidst the chaos of life, a theme that has been recurring in my recent entries.

By maintaining a musical diary, you create a personalized resource that not only fleshes out the purpose of your guitar composition but also serves as a treasure trove of creative inspiration. It allows you to channel your personal experiences, emotions, and ideas into a musical narrative that is uniquely yours.

DEFINE YOUR PURPOSE AND INSPIRATION

Clarify the purpose of your composition (e.g., emotional expression, storytelling).

Clarifying the purpose of your composition is a crucial step in the creative process, as it provides a clear direction for your musical expression and helps guide your decision-making throughout the composition journey. The first question to ask yourself must be *why* you are creating this composition. Having a clear 'why,' will help quickly flesh out the purpose of your composition.

Here are some additional steps and questions to consider to help you clarify the purpose of your composition, focusing on aspects like emotional expression and storytelling:

Reflect on Personal Emotions and Experiences

Consider the emotions you want to convey through your composition. Reflect on personal experiences or moments that evoke specific feelings.

Reflecting on personal emotions and experiences is a powerful way to discover the purpose of your guitar composition. Here are some questions to help guide your introspection:

What Emotion Am I Trying to Convey?

Identify the primary emotion or set of emotions you want to express in your composition. Is it joy, sadness, nostalgia, excitement, or a combination of feelings?

What Personal Experiences Have Shaped My Emotions?

Consider specific events or experiences in your life that have had a significant impact on your emotions.

How can you translate these experiences into musical elements?

Is There a Story to Tell?

If your emotions are tied to a narrative, think about how you can tell that story through your music. Are there specific moments or themes within the story that can be reflected in different sections of the composition?

How Can I Capture the Essence of a Memory?

If your composition is inspired by a memory, reflect on the sensory details associated with that memory. How can you capture the essence of that moment through the sounds and nuances of your guitar playing?

What Symbolic Elements Represent My Emotions?

Explore symbolic elements that represent your emotions or experiences. These could be metaphors, images, or concepts that you associate with the feelings you want to convey.

How Can I Translate Personal Growth or Reflection into Music?

If your composition is tied to personal growth or self-reflection, think about how you can musically represent this journey. Are there musical progressions, shifts in dynamics, or changes in tempo that can mirror personal development?

What Aspects of My Playing Style Reflect My Emotions?

Consider your playing style and techniques. Are there specific guitar techniques, scales, or chord progressions that resonate with your emotions? How can you incorporate these elements into your composition?

Am I Seeking Catharsis or Celebration?

Determine whether your composition is an outlet for catharsis, a way to process and release emotions, or a celebration of positive experiences. The purpose can vary depending on your emotional intent.

What Role Does the Guitar Play in My Emotional Expression?

Reflect on the unique qualities of the guitar and how it enhances the expression of your emotions. Are there specific features of the instrument that lend themselves well to conveying your feelings?

How Would I Like Others to Feel When Listening?

Consider the impact you want your composition to have on listeners. How do you hope they will feel when they experience your music? Understanding this can help shape the purpose of your composition.

Also, consider the listener's perspective. How can you create a connection between the listener and the story you're telling? What elements will make the narrative relatable or emotionally resonant?

Remember that the purpose of your composition can evolve as you explore these questions, and it's perfectly normal for your initial ideas to transform during the creative process. Allow yourself the freedom to express your emotions authentically through your music.

Identify the Story or Theme

Determine if your composition will tell a story or convey a particular theme. Think about the narrative or message you want to communicate through your music.

Consider whether there's a specific event, concept, or idea that inspired the composition.

Identifying the story or theme of your guitar composition is a crucial step in defining its purpose.

Here are some questions to help you uncover and articulate the narrative or theme behind your composition:

What Inspired Me to Create This Composition?

Consider the initial spark or inspiration behind your desire to create this piece. Is there a specific event, experience, or thought that triggered your creative process?

Is There a Personal Story I Want to Tell?

Explore the possibility of weaving a personal story into your composition. Is there a narrative from your own life that you would like to share through your music?

Do I Want to Convey a Specific Message or Lesson?

Think about whether there's a message or lesson you'd like to convey through your composition. What do you want listeners to take away from the experience?

Are There Specific Characters or Elements in the Story?

Consider whether your composition involves characters, places, or specific elements that contribute to the narrative. How can these be represented musically?

What Emotions Are Central to the Story?

Identify the core emotions associated with the story or theme. Are there moments of joy, sadness, conflict, resolution, or a mix of emotions that you want to express? An emotions dictionary is often helpful in getting in touch with emotions that seem elusive.

Does the Story Have a Clear Beginning, Middle, and End?

Structure your composition by thinking about a beginning that introduces the theme, a middle that develops the narrative, and an end that provides resolution or closure. How can you reflect this structure musically?

How Can I Use Musical Elements to Portray the Plot?

Explore how musical elements such as tempo, dynamics, rhythm, and harmony can be used to represent different aspects of the story. Can you create musical motifs that symbolize key events or characters?

Are There Symbolic Motifs or Imagery I Want to Include?

Consider incorporating symbolic motifs or imagery into your composition. These can add depth and meaning to the narrative. What musical symbols or motifs might represent key elements in the story?

Is the Composition Reflective of a Specific Genre or Style?

Think about whether the story suggests a particular musical genre or style. How can you use stylistic elements to enhance the storytelling aspect of your composition?

Does the Theme Allow for Instrumental Exploration?

If you're focusing on a theme rather than a narrative, think about how the theme lends itself to instrumental exploration. Are there unique musical aspects you can explore to bring out the essence of the theme?

By asking yourself these questions, you'll be able to delve deeper into the narrative or theme of your composition, helping you define its purpose and guide your creative choices. Remember that the process is iterative, and you may revisit and refine your ideas as your composition evolves.

Define the Atmosphere or Mood

Choose the overall mood or atmosphere you wish to create. This could be contemplative, energetic, peaceful, dramatic, etc.

Think about the sonic characteristics that align with your chosen mood, such as tempo, dynamics, and harmonic choices.

Defining the atmosphere or mood of your guitar composition is essential for creating a cohesive and evocative musical piece. Here are some questions to guide you in this process:

What Inspired the Mood I'm Trying to Create?

Refer to the sources of inspiration for the mood you want to convey. Further contemplating the inspiration can help you translate it into musical elements.

How Can I Use Dynamics to Enhance Emotional Impact?

Explore how dynamic contrasts (loudness and softness) can contribute to the mood. Are there moments in your composition where changing dynamics can enhance emotional impact?

Does the Choice of Key Contribute to the Atmosphere?

Experiment with different keys to see how they affect the overall mood. Some keys are associated with brightness, while others may have a more somber or mysterious quality.

What Role Does Tempo Play in Conveying Mood?

Consider the tempo of your composition. Does a faster tempo create a sense of energy and excitement, while a slower tempo conveys calmness or introspection? How can you use tempo changes to add variety?

Is There a Specific Time Signature That Fits the Mood?

Explore different time signatures to see how they impact the mood. Some time signatures may create a sense of stability, while others can introduce complexity or unpredictability. For example, how does a switch from 4/4 to 6/8, for example, impact the overall groove?

Are There Specific Chord Progressions That Evoke the Intended Emotion?

Experiment with different chord progressions to find ones that resonate with the mood you want to create. Minor chords, for example, are often associated with melancholy, while major chords can convey a brighter tone.

Does Instrumentation Influence the Atmosphere?

Consider the instrumentation you're using. How do different instruments or effects contribute to the overall atmosphere? Can you use a combination of acoustic and electric guitars, or incorporate other instruments to enhance the mood?

How Will Transitions Impact the Flow of Mood?

Think about how transitions between sections of your composition can impact the flow of mood. Smooth transitions can maintain a consistent atmosphere, while abrupt changes can create contrast.

By addressing these questions, you'll be able to define the atmosphere and mood of your guitar composition more clearly, enabling you to shape your music with intention and impact.

Explore Genre and Style

Consider the genre and style that best suits your intended purpose. Different genres evoke distinct emotions and storytelling approaches.

Experiment with elements from various genres to create a unique blend that aligns with your vision.

Exploring genre and style is a crucial aspect of defining the identity of your guitar composition.

Here are some questions to help you navigate and make informed decisions about the genre and style of your piece:

What Genres Am I Drawn To?
Consider the genres of music that resonate with you. Are there specific genres that inspire you or that you enjoy listening to? This can be a good starting point for defining the direction of your composition.

Am I Open to Fusion or Hybrid Styles?
Explore the possibility of blending multiple genres or creating a hybrid style. Are there interesting combinations that align with your vision for the composition?

Does My Composition Have a Cultural Influence or Fusion?

If you have cultural influences you want to incorporate, think about how they can manifest in your composition. Are there specific musical elements, scales, or rhythms from a particular culture that you find intriguing?

What Styles Complement the Guitar's Characteristics?

Consider the unique qualities of the guitar. Are there styles that naturally complement the instrument's timbre, resonance, and expressive capabilities?

Is My Composition Vocal or Instrumental, and How Does That Affect Style?

Decide whether your composition will have vocals or be purely instrumental. This choice can significantly impact the style, as vocal-driven pieces often align with specific genres and structures.

What Era or Time Period Influences My Composition?

Reflect on whether your composition is influenced by a specific era or time period. Are there musical elements from certain decades or historical periods that you want to incorporate?

Does My Composition Align with a Subgenre?

Explore subgenres within broader musical categories. Are there specific subgenres that capture the essence of your composition more accurately? This can help you narrow down your stylistic choices.

What Role Does Melody Play in Defining Style?

Consider the melodic elements of your composition. Are there specific melodic characteristics associated with the style you're aiming for? How can you use melody to reinforce the chosen genre?

Am I Incorporating Elements of Improvisation?

Decide if you want to include improvisational elements in your composition. Improvisation is often associated with certain styles, such as jazz or blues, and can influence the overall feel of your piece.

What Is the Energy Level I Want to Convey?

Consider the energy level you want your composition to have. Is it high-energy, laid-back, intense, or serene? This can guide your decisions on instrumentation, tempo, and overall arrangement.

Have I Explored Unconventional Approaches to Style?

Challenge yourself to think outside conventional genre boundaries. Are there innovative or unconventional approaches to style that align with your creative vision?

By addressing these questions, you'll be able to explore and define the genre and style of your guitar composition, allowing you to create a piece that authentically represents your artistic vision.

Experiment and Play

Allow yourself the freedom to experiment with different musical elements. Play around with melodies, harmonies, rhythms, and dynamics to see what resonates with your intended purpose.

Don't be afraid to take creative risks and explore new territories. Experimentation and play are essential aspects of the creative process for a guitar composition.

Here are some questions to help guide your exploration and experimentation:

What Happens If I Modify the Tempo?

Experiment with different tempos to see how they affect the overall mood and feel of your composition. Does a faster tempo create more energy, while a slower tempo brings out a sense of calmness or introspection?

How Can I Play with Dynamics to Enhance Expression?

Explore the full range of dynamics in your playing. What happens when you transition between loud and soft passages? How can dynamic contrasts enhance the emotional expression of your composition?

Can I Experiment with Unconventional Chord Progressions?

Break away from common chord progressions and experiment with unconventional choices. How do unique chord progressions influence the mood and atmosphere of your composition?

What If I Use Different Playing Techniques?

Try incorporating various playing techniques such as fingerpicking, hammer-ons, pull-offs, slides, and bends. How do these techniques contribute to the texture and character of your composition?

Can I Incorporate Unusual Sounds or Effects?

Explore the sonic possibilities of your guitar by incorporating effects pedals or experimenting with unconventional sounds. How can these elements add a unique flavor to your composition?

How Does Layering Multiple Guitar Parts Affect the Sound?

Experiment with layering multiple guitar parts. How do different guitar lines interact, and how does layering contribute to the complexity or richness of the composition?

What If I Change the Key or Modulate During the Piece?

Experiment with changing the key or modulating during different sections of your composition. How does this affect the overall progression and mood?

Can I Incorporate Elements of Dissonance or Tension?

Play with dissonant chords or tension-building techniques. How does introducing moments of dissonance contribute to the emotional depth of your composition?

What Happens If I Stray from Traditional Song Structures?

Break away from traditional song structures and experiment with unconventional arrangements. How does this impact the flow and unpredictability of your composition?

How Does Rhythmic Syncopation Add Interest?

Experiment with rhythmic syncopation to add a sense of groove and interest to your composition. How can irregular rhythmic patterns contribute to the overall feel?

What If I Experiment with Open Tunings?

Explore different open tunings to discover unique chord voicings and resonances. How do open tunings influence the tonal palette of your composition?

Can I Play with Silence and Pauses?

Experiment with the use of silence and intentional pauses. How does the strategic use of space contribute to the pacing and tension in your composition?

How Can I Infuse Improvisation into the Piece?

Explore opportunities for improvisation within your composition. How does incorporating spontaneous elements add a sense of freshness and unpredictability?

What If I Collaborate with Other Instruments or Musicians?

Consider collaborating with other instruments or musicians. How does the interaction between different instruments enhance the overall sonic landscape of your composition?

Remember, the process of experimentation is about being open to unexpected discoveries and embracing the joy of play. Allow yourself the freedom to explore and let your intuition guide you as you play with different elements to shape the purpose and direction of your guitar composition.

Refine Your Purpose Statement

Based on your reflections and feedback, articulate a clear purpose statement for your composition. This could be a concise sentence or set of keywords that encapsulate your intentions.

Refining your existing purpose statement for your guitar composition involves evaluating and adjusting your initial ideas.

Here are some questions to guide you through the refining process:

Is the Initial Emotion or Mood Still Relevant?

Revisit the emotion or mood you initially wanted to convey. Does it still align with your current vision for the composition, or have your ideas evolved?

Has the Story or Theme Developed Further?

If your composition is narrative-driven, consider whether the story or theme has developed or changed during the creative process. How can you refine the narrative to better align with your artistic vision?

Do Specific Musical Elements Align with the Purpose?

Evaluate the musical elements you've incorporated. Do they effectively contribute to the purpose you've outlined, or are there adjustments needed to better convey your intended message?

Have You Achieved the Technical Goals You Set?

If you had specific technical goals for your composition, assess whether you've achieved them. Are there areas where you can further refine your technique to better align with your vision?

Is the Artistic Statement Clear and Concise?

Review your artistic statement. Is it clear and concise, effectively encapsulating the purpose of your composition? Can you refine the statement to better articulate your intentions?

Has Feedback Influenced Your Purpose?

Consider any feedback you've received from others during the creative process. Have these insights influenced your purpose or provided new perspectives that you want to incorporate?

Are There Unintended Themes or Motifs That Emerged?

Sometimes, unintended themes or motifs may emerge during the creative process. Assess whether these align with or diverge from your original purpose. How can you refine or embrace these elements?

Does the Purpose Reflect Your Current Artistic Vision?

As your composition evolves, your artistic vision may develop. Evaluate whether the initial purpose still reflects your current aspirations and artistic direction.

Are There Redundancies or Excess in the Composition?

Review your composition for any redundancies or excesses that may have emerged. Are there sections that can be refined or streamlined to improve the overall cohesion of the piece?

Have You Explored Alternative Approaches to Achieve the Purpose?

Explore alternative approaches to achieve your purpose. Are there new ideas or techniques you've discovered during the process that could better serve your artistic vision?

Does the Composition Still Align with Your Personal Connection?

Reconnect with the personal aspects of your composition. Does it still resonate with you on a personal level? How can you refine the composition to deepen that connection?

Is the Purpose Consistent Throughout the Composition?

Ensure that the purpose remains consistent throughout the composition. Are there sections that deviate from the established purpose, and do these deviations contribute positively or require refinement?

Have You Considered the Composition's Long-Term Impact?

Reflect on the long-term impact you want your composition to have. Does the refined purpose align with your aspirations for the piece in terms of its lasting impression on listeners?

By asking yourself these questions, you'll be able to refine and further develop the purpose of your guitar composition, ensuring that it aligns closely with your artistic vision and intentions.

Refer back to this purpose statement as a guiding beacon throughout the composition process.

DRAW INSPIRATION FROM PERSONAL EXPERIENCES, EMOTIONS, OR EXTERNAL SOURCES

Drawing inspiration from personal experiences, emotions, or external sources is a powerful way to infuse authenticity and depth into your guitar compositions.

Reflect on Personal Experiences

Take time to reflect on your own life experiences, both significant and mundane. Consider moments of joy, sadness, love, challenges, or personal growth.

Think about events, relationships, or places that left a lasting impression on you.

Reflecting on personal experiences is a powerful way to gain inspiration for your guitar composition. Here are some questions to help you delve into your personal history and draw inspiration for your creative process:

What Personal Memories Hold Emotional Significance?

Identify specific memories from your life that hold emotional weight. These could be joyful, challenging, or introspective moments that resonate with you.

Are There Specific Life Events or Milestones That Stand Out?

Reflect on significant life events or milestones. Is there a particular moment or period that left a lasting impression on you? How can you translate the essence of these events into musical expression?

Have Relationships or Interactions Shaped Your Perspectives?

Explore the impact of relationships and interactions with others. Have personal connections, friendships, or conflicts influenced your emotions and perspectives? How can these experiences be translated into musical themes?

How Have Personal Challenges or Triumphs Shaped You?

Reflect on challenges you've faced and triumphs you've celebrated. How have these experiences shaped your character, and can you express the journey through your music?

Are There Specific Themes or Lessons You've Learned?

Identify themes or life lessons that resonate with you. What wisdom or insights have you gained from your experiences? How can these themes be woven into the narrative of your composition?

Have Personal Hobbies or Passions Inspired You?

Explore your hobbies and passions. Whether it's a love for nature, literature, art, or any other interest, think about how these pursuits can be mirrored in your musical creation.

How Can Personal Struggles or Triumphs Be Conveyed Musically?

Consider how personal struggles or triumphs can be conveyed through musical elements. Are there specific chord progressions, melodies, or dynamics that can capture the essence of your experiences?

Have Dreams or Aspirations Influenced Your Perspective?

Reflect on your dreams and aspirations. How have they influenced your perspective on life? Can you use your composition to convey the journey toward those dreams?

Do Specific Sounds or Smells Trigger Memories?

Explore sensory experiences. Are there sounds, smells, or textures that trigger vivid memories for you? How can you incorporate these sensory elements into your musical narrative?

How Can You Create a Personal Connection with Your Audience?

Consider how your personal experiences can create a connection with your audience. How can your music resonate on a universal level, inviting listeners to connect with their own personal stories?

As you answer these questions, you'll not only gain inspiration for your guitar composition but also deepen your connection with the material, making your music more authentic and emotionally resonant.

Explore Emotions Through Improvisation

Use improvisation as a tool to express your current emotions. Play freely on the guitar, allowing your feelings to guide your musical choices.

Record your improvisations to capture spontaneous moments of inspiration.

Incorporate Personal Narratives

Tell a musical story that mirrors your personal narratives. Consider structuring your composition to reflect the arc of a personal journey or experience.

Use different sections of your composition to represent various aspects of your story.

Engage with External Art and Literature

Seek inspiration from external sources such as literature, poetry, visual art, or films. Explore themes, characters, or narratives that resonate with you.

Use these external stimuli to inform the mood, atmosphere, or even specific musical elements of your composition.

Use Symbolism and Metaphors

Incorporate symbolism and metaphors into your compositions to convey deeper meanings. Translate abstract concepts into musical expressions that resonate with your personal experiences.

The key is to remain open, observant, and receptive to the world around you. The more you engage with your own experiences and the broader spectrum of art and life, the richer and more authentic your guitar compositions can become.

CREATE YOUR PURPOSE STATEMENT

Creating a purpose statement for your guitar composition involves identifying and articulating the core intentions, emotions, or themes you aim to convey through your music.

Reflect on Inspiration

Consider what inspired you to create the composition. Think about personal experiences, emotions, stories, or concepts that have influenced your creative process.

Identify Core Themes or Emotions

Identify the central themes or emotions you want to express through your composition. This could include joy, nostalgia, introspection, excitement, or any other feelings that resonate with your vision.

Define the Story or Narrative

Determine if your composition tells a story or conveys a specific narrative. If so, outline key elements of the story or the message you want to communicate through your music.

Consider Technical and Stylistic Goals

Reflect on any technical or stylistic goals you have for the composition. This could involve experimenting with specific guitar techniques, exploring a particular genre, or achieving a unique sound.

Envision the Listener's Experience

Envision how you want your audience to experience your composition. Consider the mood, atmosphere, and overall impact you aim to create for the listeners.

Craft a Clear and Concise Statement

Condense your reflections into a clear and concise purpose statement. Use language that captures the essence of your creative vision and communicates your intentions effectively.

Consider Audience Connection

Reflect on how you want your composition to connect with the audience. Consider whether your purpose statement effectively communicates to both musicians and non-musicians, depending on your target audience.

Example Purpose Statement:

[Date]

"Through my guitar composition, (Title), I aim to transport listeners to a realm of nostalgic reflection. Drawing inspiration from my own memories of bygone days, the piece unfolds like a storytelling journey, weaving intricate fingerstyle melodies with emotive chord progressions. The purpose is to evoke a sense of bittersweet nostalgia, inviting listeners to rediscover the beauty in fleeting moments and the echoes of the past. By seamlessly

blending classical influences with contemporary nuances, 'Whispers of the Past' seeks to resonate with a diverse audience, fostering a deep emotional connection and leaving a lasting imprint of shared memories."

Remember, your purpose statement is a guiding principle for your creative process. It should capture the essence of your composition and help you make informed decisions as you work on your guitar piece. Feel free to adapt the language and specifics to match your unique creative vision.

DOCUMENT YOUR CREATIVE PROCESS

In your musical diary, record your thoughts about the purpose of your composition. Document how your ideas evolve over time and the decisions you make to align with your intended purpose.

Documenting your creative process for a guitar composition is a valuable practice that can help you track your journey, gain insights, and revisit your thought processes.

Here are some questions to ask yourself as you document your creative process:

What Inspired Me to Start This Composition?

Reflect on the initial spark that led you to start working on this composition. Was it a specific emotion, experience, story, or concept?

How Did I Begin?

Describe the first steps you took in creating the composition. Did you start with a melody, a chord progression, or a specific idea?

What Were My Initial Goals or Intentions?

Document the goals or intentions you set for the composition when you started. This could include technical objectives, emotional impact, or stylistic choices.

How Did I Develop the Melody and Harmony?

Detail the process of developing the melody and harmony. How did you choose the notes and chords? Were there specific musical elements that influenced your decisions?

Did I Experiment with Different Tunings or Techniques?

Note any experimentation with guitar tunings, playing techniques, or effects. How did these experiments contribute to the overall sound of your composition?

Were There Challenges or Roadblocks?

Document any challenges or obstacles you encountered during the creative process. How did you overcome them, and did they lead to unexpected breakthroughs?

Did I Collaborate with Others?

If you collaborated with other musicians or sought feedback, describe the collaboration process. How did external input influence your creative choices?

How Did the Composition Evolve Over Time?

Track the evolution of your composition. Did the initial ideas change, and how did you adapt or refine them as the piece developed?

What Were the Key Decisions I Made Along the Way?

Identify the key decisions you made during the creative process. These could include choices related to structure, instrumentation, dynamics, or mood.

How Did I Approach Transitions Between Sections?

Detail your approach to transitioning between different sections of the composition. How did you ensure smooth transitions and maintain coherence?

Did I Revisit and Revise Sections?

Discuss any instances where you revisited and revised sections of the composition. What prompted these revisions, and how did they enhance the overall piece?

How Did I Conclude the Composition?

Describe your approach to concluding the composition. Did you use a specific technique or motif to bring the piece to a resolution?

What Feedback Did I Receive, and How Did I Respond?

Document any feedback you received from others. How did you respond to constructive criticism, and did it lead to changes in your approach?

How Do I Feel About the Final Outcome?

Reflect on your emotions and satisfaction with the final outcome. How closely does the composition align with your initial intentions, and are you content with the result?

By actively engaging in these steps, you can clarify the purpose of your composition, whether it's centered around emotional expression, storytelling, or any other creative objective. This clarity not only guides your composition process but also resonates with listeners, creating a meaningful and intentional musical experience.

What Did I Learn from This Creative Process?

Summarize the lessons and insights gained from the creative process. What aspects of your approach would you carry forward into future compositions?

CLOSING

In closing, we extend our heartfelt congratulations to you for embarking on this musical journey with *A Guitarist's Grimoire: Unlocking the Secrets of Creating A Musical Diary To Master Guitar Composition*. Through the pages of this comprehensive guide, we've explored the intricate art of cultivating a musical diary, delving into the vast realm of creativity and craftsmanship that defines a guitarist's true potential.

As you reflect upon the wealth of knowledge shared in these chapters, consider the profound transformation that awaits you as a musician. Your newfound understanding of the importance of creating a musical diary serves as a key to unlock the doors of inspiration, allowing you to navigate the vast landscape of guitar composition with confidence and innovation.

From the initial steps of crafting your musical diary to exploring various approaches and best practices, we've provided you with a roadmap to illuminate your path. Your musical diary entries, carefully curated and nurtured, now stand as testaments to your unique voice in the language of music. The sources of inspiration and ideas we've uncovered together serve as a wellspring of creativity, ensuring that your compositions are not merely notes on a page but living expressions of your soul.

Through the exploration of dreams and aspirations, you've learned to infuse your music with personal meaning and significance, transcending the boundaries of technique to touch the hearts and minds of those who will be fortunate enough to experience your compositions. The incorporation of visual elements into your musical diary adds an extra layer of depth, making your creations not only audible but visually evocative.

Now, armed with your enriched musical diary, you are poised to use it as a perpetual source for your ongoing compositions. Your diary is not a static record but a dynamic reservoir, ready to inspire and guide you through the ever-evolving landscape of your artistic endeavors.

As you continue on your musical odyssey, remember that every note you play is a brushstroke on the canvas of your unique musical identity. Embrace the challenges, celebrate the triumphs, and cherish the creative process as a lifelong companion. Your guitar is not just an instrument; it is a vessel for your emotions, dreams, and stories.

May the pages of *A Guitarist's Grimoire* remain dog-eared and well-loved, serving as a constant source of inspiration as you navigate the rich tapestry of your musical pursuits. Thank you for entrusting us with your creative aspirations, and may your guitar continue to be the faithful companion in your ever-evolving musical diary.

Play on, create fearlessly, and let the magic of your musical journey unfold.

If you enjoyed this book, please consider spreading your good word. Thank you!

INDEX